PRINT IN FASHION

MARNIE FOGG
PRINT IN FASHION

DESIGN AND DEVELOPMENT
IN FASHION TEXTILES

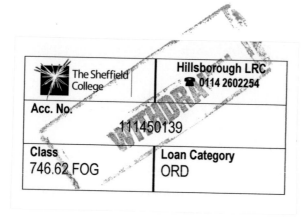
First Published 2006

Text © Marnie Fogg 2006

The right of Marnie Fogg to be identified as Author of this work has been asserted by her in accordance with the Copyright, Designs and Patents Act 1988.

Illustrations © of the designers specified (see picture credits)

ISBN 07134 9012 8
(13 digit) 9780713490121

A CIP catalogue record for this book is available from the British Library.

Printed in China

for the publishers

B T Batsford
The Chrysalis Building
Bramley Road
London W10 6SP

www.batsford.com

Volume © B T Batsford 2006

Distributed in the United States and Canada by Sterling Publishing Co., 387 Park Avenue South, New York, NY 10016, USA

contents

1 print into fashion   6

2 'and, next to nature, art'   24

3 abstract   62

4 folklore, fantasy and fable   100

5 graphics and graffiti   128

6 vintage   156

footnotes 178

bibliography 180

index 182

acknowledgements 187

picture credits 189

chapter one
print into fashion

The relationship between print and high fashion has never been more potent. To decorate the human body is a natural instinct; the desire to embellish ourselves and the world around us is intrinsic to the human experience, and one that is denied when the decorative tradition is discarded. For more than thirty years print has been used to support the concepts of structure and shape, designers adhering to the modernist precepts that form follows function and that decoration for its own sake is somehow essentially frivolous.

Print in fashion is rarely connected to performance, which is reason enough for its detractors to consider it as less than cerebral. If it has no function, however, then its virtues are to do with the joy of the unnecessary. Print is a distraction and yet invites recognition; it is an affirmation that there is time in the world to play, and that decoration is, in itself, a purpose. According to Martin Raymond, editor of *Viewpoint* magazine and co-founder of Future Laboratory, it is technology that has allowed designers to reinvent this sense of play. 'New ways of printing are challenging how we understand print.'

For Consuelo Castiglioni of the Italian label Marni print has been important since the inception of the label in 1994. 'Prints are not a recent trend for me, they have been a distinctive characteristic of my collection from the beginning. I see this general drift towards print as a reaction to formal constraints, I feel this might be a tendency of the moment because of a diffused search for an eclectic, upbeat and fun fashion.' To the question of whether print and cut serve different ideals there is no single answer. For Castiglioni, one enhances the other. 'My goal is to achieve harmony between colour and shape. Structural design becomes decoration and produces a new form and function.' Other fashion designers who work with print also reject absolutely the idea that it is an 'add on', or an afterthought. The most obvious assumption is that print comes before the garment, but that is not always the case. Sometimes the print is the garment. Certainly the design on the cloth has to be related to the cut of the cloth if the garment is to have any sort of authenticity. Christopher Bailey, creative director of global class brand Burberry, and responsible for its upscale catwalk collection Prorsum, summarizes: 'I feel that for fashion and clothing you need to fuse the worlds of cut and

colour and print and neither stands alone if it is to be worn on the body. Otherwise it becomes a purely artistic expression as opposed to an emotional/functional point of view.'

Fashion is fuelled by the desire for change, and pattern and colour are now a desirable aesthetic. Designers are eager to harness the convenience of new technology, but never for the sake of novelty. Many prefer to utilize those screen-printing skills learned in the art college workshop, where most experimentation takes place. These innovations in technique and design, and the joyful adoption of colour, pattern and texture, are lending themselves to a radical shift in fashion in the 21st century. There is a new softness, a more complicated sexiness and a concern with volume that readily lends itself to the use of print. The turn of the 20th century saw the explosion of fashion into colour and texture with the work of the great couturier Paul Poiret. As fashion progresses into the new millennium, it is Poiret's mannered extravagance that is inspiring contemporary designers. Raymond believes that 'we are in revolt against minimalism; the 80s were black, the 90s oatmeal and beige. Consumers were brought up with minimalism, and now they are ready for something new. They have re-embraced the notions of maximalism. The developments in print, texture and finish wouldn't have worked in a 90s context.'

The invention of the screen-printing process was instrumental in providing the market with the first fashion fabrics in bulk. Samuel Simon took out the first patent for a screen-printing process in 1907. This relatively cheap and less laborious method of printing cloth accelerated the speed of response to changing fashion trends and liberated designers from the limitations of expensive block-printing methods or engraved roller machines.

Further inventions and patents followed, and by the 1930s screen-printing works were set up throughout Europe and North America. These innovations democratized print design, and revolutionized the textile printing industry, particularly for fashion fabrics.

The 1960s heralded the golden age of print in fashion. Images borrowed from Op art and Pop Art, and the psychedelic swirls of iconic fashion house Pucci, were only the beginning. They were followed by an Art Nouveau revival and the subsequent preoccupation with Art Deco, the latter inspired by Bernard Nevill, then professor of textiles at the Royal College of Art and head of print at the influential London store

Opposite: the Marni label has consistently pioneered the use of print. The softly sculptured volume of this high-waisted skirt and cropped jacket reflect the Mannerist influence of 20th-century couturier Poiret. Previous page: 'Beauty Bar' (see page 13).

Liberty. The hippie culture, with its plethora of peacock feathers and paisleys, was followed in quick succession through the 1960s and early 1970s by the innovative prints of Zandra Rhodes, and Bill Gibb. The high point of that era was the collaboration between Celia Birtwell and Ossie Clark, who together provided the perfect synthesis between print and fashion.

The British recession that followed the entrepreneurial 1960s secured the place of the minimalist American designers in the fashion hierarchy. Calvin Klein and Donna Karan eschewed the role of the decorative print, producing modern, simple clothes that took their influence from sportswear and reflected the changing role of women in the workplace.

Fashion's preoccupation with power-dressing in the 1980s resulted in tailored dressing for women, which was opposed by the conceptual and intellectual rigour of Japanese designers such as Yohji Yamamoto and Rei Kawakubo, the latter associated with the label Commes des Garcons, which she founded in 1973. Print was confined to the margins; Vivienne Westwood produced her pirate collection in 1981, an amalgamation of earthy African colours that juxtaposed prints of various scales and subjects. It was the age of the declamatory T-shirt for designers such as Katherine Hamnett, while Hilde Smith combined high-contrast prints with jacquard knits for the Bodymap label. Fleet Bigwood, director of corporate print development for American fashion label Donna Karan – as well as running his own design studio in partnership with Brigitte Appleyard – remembers that 'print was much more graphic and experimental then, probably because of the new interest and innovations in graphic design by people like Neville Brody in book and magazine publishing.' At the couture end of the market, Italian designer Gianni Versace introduced his signature style of ostentatious glamour, decadent prints in luxurious fabrics that sold in the most exclusive boutiques in the world.

During the 1990s print was integral to the promulgation of a conceptual approach within the avant-garde aesthetic. Martin Margiela designed garments printed with the marks customarily seen on paper pattern pieces in his 1996 collection, which deconstructed the haute couture process. Others used anarchic imagery and text to subvert and interrupt the fashion process. However, this was print concerned with the message rather than the medium. Mainstream fashion was preoccupied with conveying sexy, hard-edged glamour, such as Tom Ford's designs for luxury label Gucci. His monochromatic palette defined late-20th century metropolitan minimalism. Phillip de Leon, designer with the Californian print company Alexander Henry Fabrics, recalls, 'I remember one fall in the mid 90s when it seemed every woman on the street was wearing black pants, a black coat and high leather boots. I was in New York and the city looked positively occupied by this fashion army!'

It is only now, in the 21st century, that printed textiles have taken centre stage; those designers who have always relished the art of decoration have now found that rather than being peripheral to the prevailing fashion ethos, they are pivotal to it. Fleet Bigwood recalls, 'When I started my print studio in the 1990s, it was a combination of print and silhouette and applying texture to an architectural form. Prints are now part of everything and have become integral to the way collections are put together; hugely scaled or engineered. Now it is all about pattern.' As the black trouser suit becomes the ubiquitous cliché of business culture, power dressing is now about breaking the rules, allowing a softer, more individual approach to fashion in the business hierarchy. Glimpses of colour and pattern can even be seen in the boardroom as women have consolidated their management role and no longer require camouflage against the backdrop of their suited male co-workers. Fleet Bigwood concurs: 'I think today's "touchy-feely" society has morphed into pattern in the fashion world.'

Bigwood has worked with many of the major fashion designers and labels, from Jill Sander, Narciso Rodriguez and Aquascutum to Jasper Conran and Cacharel. 'The designer initiates and drives the process; we see ourselves as the facilitators. We interpret the designer's handwriting, and personality. For instance, Giles Deacon likes to play technically; Phoebe Philo of Chloe is fascinated by the processes and is very intuitive. Jasper Conran is about colour on cloth.'

This enormous resurgence of interest in print design has seen most major international designers incorporating print into their collections, and its popularity is also reflected in the mass market. This is confirmed by Nicole de Leon and her brother Phillip, of design house Alexander Henry Fabrics, who not only produce two new collections annually with their father Marc de Leon, but also market their own fabrics world-wide. The company has distributors in Canada, Australia and Europe, as well as

Japan, where most of the printing takes place. With designs featured in the New York Textile museum, the company sells prints to a diverse range of clients, from cutting-edge designers to large corporate manufacturers around the world. According to Phillip de Leon, there are no longer significant differences in print preferences globally. 'Print designers are now speaking a more common language due to the unifying technologies of television and the internet. There is less difference because we are all looking at the same things, tracking the same trends.' In the face of a globally connected culture, this shared language is a way of expressing individuality through the use of print. Nicole de Leon asserts: 'There will always be fashion edicts, but these are more fleeting than ever before. What is the ultimate fashion edict now? Be yourself. Prints have always underscored individuality, and have been a way of saying, "I chose to express myself by wearing this".'

Multiple retailers and department stores exist in almost every high street and shopping centre, and companies such as Spanish label Zara offer an almost instant take on big-label names. Jane Shepherdson, brand director of highly respected British fashion chain Topshop, is one of the most influential women in British fashion today. 'Over the last four years every type of print has been popular, from florals to spots, to abstracts, to tribal – and right now, the bolder the better! A print will sell a garment, regardless of whether or not the style is perfect.' Although equally admiring of both Marni and Dries van Noten for their ability to transmute print into fashion, Shepherdson affirms her belief in British designers: 'We certainly have a lot of great print designers, but we also have the best designers in the world, too. I've always thought it was because we have a great irreverence, and are keen to break the rules, which engenders new ideas.'

Shepherdson recognizes that the desire for colour, pattern and texture is due in part to the cyclical nature of fashion, and accounts for the current revival of interest in the print designs of Celia Birtwell, Pucci and Zandra Rhodes. She acknowledges that new technologies have also had an impact on the popularity of print. 'The quality of print we can now produce is much better than it was, and the use of CAD [computer-aided design] has made it much easier to reproduce and recolour prints.'

Designing prints for fashion offers unique challenges. Scale has to be defined by the parameters of the body, and pattern can either accentuate or diffuse the lines of the garment, disguising or redefining the body beneath. This is evident in the work of Mark Eley and Wakako Kishimoto, who make up design label Eley Kishimoto, among the forerunners of the pattern revival. Consuelo Castiglioni for Marni and Konstantin Kakanias for Yves Saint Laurent and Christian Lacroix are similarly responsible for the integration of print design into the identity of those labels. Both Italian design house Etro and Belgian designer Dries van Noten are renowned for the symbiotic relationship between garment and print in their designs.

Some design labels buy in print ideas, either from a high-profile textile designer, or from a studio showing at one of the trade fairs such as Premier Vision. This is a commercial marketing organization dedicated to promoting the textile industry and hosts to up to 800 fashion fabric manufacturers from around the world displaying and selling their work. Val Furphy of the Furphy Simpson Studio remarks, 'Some designers are secretive about buying in prints – they like customers to think that [the designers themselves] are responsible or that they are done in house. Textile designers get so little credit.' Ian Simpson and Val Furphy, both 1976 graduates of the Royal College of Art, have successfully sold fashion prints to all levels of the industry from couture to high street. Some of the first designers to work directly on cloth rather than on paper, they specialize in discharge printing – the bleaching out of a lighter colour from a darker ground. Each season their studio produces at least 300 samples. 'The difference now from when we started out is that we work far closer to the season and not so much in advance. There is also a trend for fabric manipulation. Print is not enough. Now we add to the mix embroidery, pleating, distressing and bonding.'

Fleet Bigwood admires this ability to sustain such a level of output, but himself prefers a more direct involvement with the fashion industry. 'I wanted to be involved in fashion rather than sell swatches on because I wanted to see the end product. It's

Opposite: *Alexander Henry Fabrics specialise in 'conversational prints' and designs that offer a quirky narrative in terms of subject matter. Here, components of a dressing table make up the design 'Beauty Bar'.*

13

very self-indulgent because I get the chance to experiment and play, using sanding machines on tarnished and stained leathers, or burning images into [a] wool jersey. We'll try anything and see what it does.'

Digital printing can take an image directly from camera or computer screen to cloth in one step, eliminating countless colour separations and freeing the designer from the labour-intensive and costly practices of conventional silk-screen printing. However, for some designers these traditional, painstaking methods are an intrinsic element of the creative process. For Australian-born designer Megan Park, the time she spends with the artisans in Delhi who handblock-print her textiles is integral to the outcome of the design.

Of the initial studio process, Nicole de Leon of Alexander Henry Fabrics explains, 'We are painters, and we love to paint, and the fact that the process is organic. We use watercolour, luma dye and gouache primarily, and moving and blending the colour are vital to the process.' Phillip de Leon concurs: 'As a company we feel tied to the tradition of textile design. There is an intimacy to our finished product that does not go unnoticed. When we present a collection, our clients approach each painted piece as something original, where the hand of the artist is definitely in evidence. You don't have this kind of emotional experience with digitally produced work.'

Right: *The bleaching out of a lighter colour from a darker ground still requires the screen-printing process. These two designs from discharge print specialist Furphy–Simpson Studio are on crepe satin.* Opposite: *hand-crafted embellishment combined with print by Megan Park.*

Above: *the first glimpse of a new design on cloth as print designer Fleet Bigwood lifts the silk screen stencil at the sample print table in his studio.* Opposite: *With his partner Brigitte Appleyard, the designer checks the initial strike off for accuracy before committing to the production of a sample length.*

Wakako Kishimoto of Eley Kishimoto has a similar view. 'I like the purity of the handcrafted process. It's part of the rhythm of working, and creates a mental space.' Fleet Bigwood describes the physicality of the process as 'primitive'. 'I'm a traditionalist. With me it's about lifting the screen. Only when I lift the screen does it get exciting. Sometimes I work on fabric in the piece, developing artwork directly onto film to produce one-off pieces. That's how I develop ideas for Donna Karan. She oversees all aspects of the design process. I see her for about an hour each season, we have a couple of conversations and I go away and start playing. Once the artwork is complete I make a screen and play with colour, dimension and scale. One screen creates infinite variations. Our studio is very much like a college set-up, with three or four people and a 5-metre print table.' In his role as lecturer to students at Central St Martins School of Art in London, he ensures that traditional methods are passed on. 'Experimental techniques always start out in the college studio; only then are they adopted commercially. The craft process is important, and as a teacher I encourage that process – the union of brain, hand and eye. You have to take on board that ink-jet is just a colour copy. You're very often saying, " Look what I can do. Oh, I've done it."'

In contrast, fashion newcomers Basso & Brooke rely completely on technology, as Bruno Basso explains. 'We are 100 per cent digital, we have no romantic ideas about the processes of printmaking.'

Digital printing is often thought by some designers to produce inferior results to traditional methods. Magnus Mighall, representing R A Smart, one of Britain's largest suppliers of traditional screen-printing equipment as well as of the latest digital technology, admits that in the early days quality might have been an issue. 'When digital printing first came out a digital print could be spotted a mile off. It was very obviously doing things that only digital could do. We are now moving away from that, and the next five years will see some amazing advances, particularly in dye development.'

Mighall is an enthusiastic champion of digital printing. 'Constraints have disappeared – short runs for screen printing were cost prohibitive – and also with digital printing scale is not a factor. Neither is it labour-intensive: one person can run three or four printers at the same time. It could be the opportunity to bring the printing business back into Britain.' He believes digital printing will become increasingly cost effective. 'Digital inks are expensive compared to traditional

pigments, as suppliers needed to recoup their research and development costs. It took a long time to develop a good textile ink to go through the print heads and gain momentum so that the dye stuff had the right depth of colour and "runability".'

Although digitally printed fabric still needs to be steamed and washed, the speed of the printing process far exceeds that of screen printing, though not of rotary printing. 'The fashion industry really lends itself to digital printing, which is short run, high expense. At the high end of the market we will use a lower speed, which increases the quality of the print, and print 10–15 square metres an hour. We can do up to 50 square metres an hour.'

Patricia Belford is a senior research fellow at the University of Ulster, and the co-director of Belford Prints Ltd. Since setting up her business in 1986 she has been at the forefront of international print design, responsible for the research and development of all print concepts, from testing and sampling through to production, for designers such as Donna Karan, Matthew Williamson, Betty Jackson, Calvin Klein and Vivienne Westwood. When Belford started her business it was the only facility outside Italy prepared to do the sophisticated and expensive minimum-length quality dye printing using reactive acid dyes, rather than the straightforward process

Above: *Automatic printed fabric production without the need for screen preparation at R.A. Smarts, using Mimaki TX-series digital plotters.* Opposite: *Print design 'La Folia', using digital printing by Basso & Brooke from their collection 'The Succubus and other Tales'.*

Above: *The print table in preparation for a print run at Belford Prints Ltd., England. Stop blocks are fixed to the side rail to provide accurate colour registration.*

of pigment dyeing. 'Pigment dyeing stays on the surface of the cloth, which is fine for things like T-shirts, but I always think, "how can I change the fabric?"'

Belford was responsible for reintroducing to the fashion industry the technique of devore printing, which was eagerly seized upon by Jasper Conran and Donna Karan and soon saturated the mass market. 'In 1998, production of devoré moved to China. This is increasingly true of all printing, and we have to be philosophical about it and move on. China gives the deliveries, the price and the quality, but not the look, so we have to concentrate on the creative side, on sampling and prototypes.'

She fears that with the onset of digital printing, some of that creativity may be lost. 'With digital printing, designers don't need to know anything about print. I don't

like getting an image from a designer just to scan it and send back the printed cloth. Using the latest digital technology my role now is to research and investigate the impact of digital media and new technologies within the broad area of international textiles. My mission is to put the creativity back into printing.' To this end she prefers a dialogue with the designer. 'When I work with designers such as Neisha Crosland I will show her a technique such as selectively shrinking part of the cloth, and Neisha thinks about what she would then like to do with it.'

This mixing of print processes allows the designer to retain a close connection with the cloth. 'I like the alchemy of fabric. The rainbow print for Matthew Williamson was printed digitally and then screen-printed with foil, as the digital printer cannot yet process metallics.' The limitations in the digital print system include an inability

Above: *Following the silk screen's exposure to U.V. light, a single colour component stencil of the design is revealed by washing off the exposed emulsion. Checks are made for pinholes and other defects in the screen.*

Above: *discharge printing using single operative print carriage at Belford Prints Ltd. After placement of the silk screen, discharge paste is 'squeegeed' onto the dark fabric prior to treatment, which chemically removes the existing pigment.*

to do discharge printing, which is essential for the manufacture of high-quality scarves and ties. For this reason up to 30 screens are required for a scarf design for the luxury-goods label Asprey.

With 'smart' dyes, such as thermochromic inks that respond to atmospheric conditions by changing colour, designs on plain fabrics that mutate into a pattern when wet, and even pigments carrying miniature solar cells capable of harvesting sunlight, print design for fashion enables the body to become uniquely interactive with the outer world.

Although contemporary print design may benefit from the underlying technical processes, image-making and the development of a visual vocabulary by the designer is always intrinsic to creative activity. Innovative techniques are a means to an end, whether they are the prints engineered to fit each pattern piece by designer Jonathan Saunders, or the complex hand-drawn prints of Julie Verhoeven's multi-layered images for Italian company Gibo.

This book is concerned with all aspects of the design process, and will examine sources of inspiration, preferred methods of working and studio practices employed by contemporary cutting-edge designers. It will consider the role of innovative developments in print technology and how the immediacy of modern processes affects creativity, maintaining the sublime conjunction of image, colour and texture that printed textiles for fashion represent.

Above: *Discharge printing can remove a dischargeable colour from a fabric and replace it with another 'illuminating' colour. Although photorealist digital printing is plotted directly onto fabric, it still has to be steamed, washed and pressed to achieve the permanent finished effect.*

chapter two

'and, next to nature, art'

Human beings have always had a desire to replicate images of the natural world. From flowers and animals to landscapes, the organic continues to animate and inspire designers. Whether representations of nature are found in the overtly seductive animal prints of Italian duo Dolce & Gabbana, Matthew Williamson's exuberant interpretation of the peacock feather, or the crisp lively florals of Ann-Louise Roswald, print design in the 21st century celebrates the beauty of nature in an attempt to reconnect with a freshness and innocence seemingly lacking in modern life.

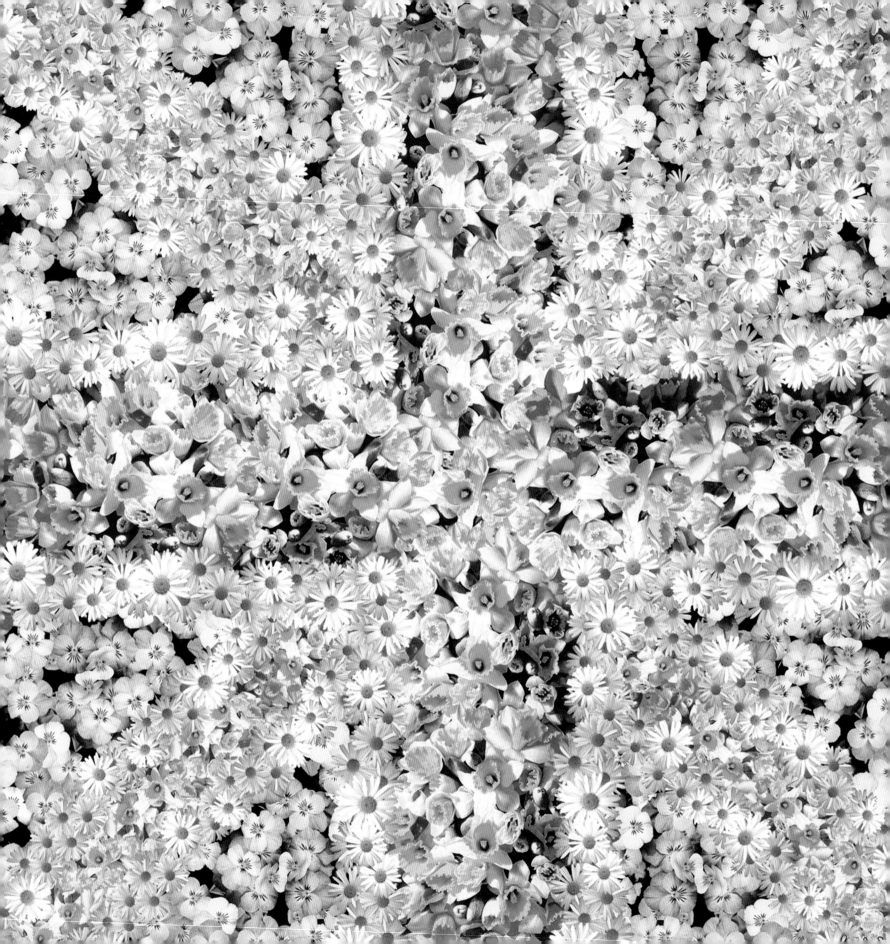

'Nature I loved and, next to nature, art.'

W S Landor (1775–1864)

The appreciation of flowers is part of that universal yearning for a pastoral idyll that evokes the simplicity of a sun-filled childhood spent running through meadows. In the frenetic pace of modern urban life, city dwellers tend to feel progressively more alienated from nature, and so seek solace in a romanticized rural ideal. Marc Jacobs commissioned botanical illustrator Amanda Griffiths to design the fabrics for his summer 2002 collection, featuring some of the plant and animal life she had found in a Hampshire field, including honeysuckle, fritillaries, cow parsley and butterflies. Flowers are romantic – they are given both to charm and to appease – and these associations are drawn on when they appear, for instance, on a watchband from Gucci's summer 2005 collection. This features the 'Flora' print, found in the archives by Gucci's head of accessories, Frida Giannini; it had originally been designed as a headscarf for Princess Grace in 1966 by Rodolfo Gucci and the artist Vittorio Accornero.

The decorative use of nature reached its apotheosis in England's Elizabethan era, when the love of flowers, celebrated in the literature of Spenser, Sidney and Shakespeare, was also represented in interiors and in dress. This can be seen as an attempt to bring the garden indoors, though the floral designs were embroidered or woven rather than printed. It was the importing in the 17th century of patterned, block-printed 'calicoes' – the name derives from the Indian port of Calicut, now Kozhikode – that established the European decorative tradition of floral printed cloth as fashionable wear. Once the English East India Company was granted its charter in 1600, Western merchants were able to commission their own versions of floral designs, bringing a European sensibility to the Indian craft. Daniel Defoe observed in the *Weekly Review* of 1708: 'The general fansie of the people runs upon East India goods to that degree, that the chintz and painted calicoes, which before were only made use of for carpets, quilts etc., and to clothe children and ordinary people, become now the dress of our ladies, and such is the power of a mode as we saw our persons of quality dressed in Indian carpets, which but a few years before would have thought too ordinary for them.'[i]

Previous page: 'Abstract Rose' printed on raw silk by Ann-Louise Roswald. Opposite and pages 28–29: Paul Smith references his connection to the British love of flowers with a series of images and print designs for a scarf.

THE EARTHLY PARADISE

Flowers as a source of inspiration continue to be part of the designers' vocabulary, interpreted according to the prevailing ethos of the time. William Morris, the leading member of the Arts and Crafts movement, upheld this preoccupation with nature as a source of inspiration in the 19th century. Victorian Britain was the world's first urbanized society, and within the confines of its cities chaos and danger were feared to lie, in contrast to the perceived safety and serenity of an idealized countryside.[ii] For Americans in this period, by contrast, danger was felt to lie outside the cities in a wilderness that needed to be tamed. Perhaps that is why in European culture a love of flowers is traditionally expressed in a naturalistic way, to calm and soothe.

As a reaction to the mechanization of the Industrial Revolution and the stiff, stylized floral motifs intrinsic to Victorian design, William Morris reintroduced the notion of the artist-craftsman, producing block-printed floral designs initially for use in interiors. His prints continue to undergo periods of revival, and have repeatedly been used for fashion, whether on a 1960s miniskirt or a 21st-century dress. The London store Liberty has an equally enduring relationship with the floral tradition. Opened in 1875 by Arthur Lasenby Liberty, the shop initially imported textiles from India and Japan, but was one of the first stores to commission designers directly. At the end of the 19th century Liberty became one of the foremost proselytizers of Art Nouveau, a design movement that transcended nature to produce sinuous, sensuous forms, and which thrived throughout Western Europe and North America. During the 20th century the tradition continued, from the psychedelic swirls of 1960s 'flower power' to the vibrant, large-scale poppies of the Finnish company Marimekko. As designer Celia Birtwell remarks, 'Nature always comes into the equation.'

Paul Smith

Trend forecaster Li Edelkoort is convinced that this desire to recreate a modern Eden of plant images is not a temporary phenomenon. 'The plant and flower boom is more than just a passing craze. The sensuality of plants is reassuring; their very presence is a small victory against ambient noise and visual pollution … perfect antidotes for daily stress and cybernetic non-existence. Since we don't want to leave our gardens behind when we finish toiling, we take them with us, thanks to our garments.'[iii]

This great delight and urgency in consolidating our desire for a connection with our rural roots is also connected to a contemporary awareness of environmental issues and anxieties about the world's diminishing natural resources, all of which increase the appeal of recreating fast-vanishing flora and fauna.

Turkish-Cypriot designer Hussein Chalayan is inspired by the animal kingdom, and in particular endangered species. His new line, named Chalayan after himself, is for a younger, less expensive market, and the print it features is based on a series of drawings of animals – lions, pandas, whales, swans, snakes and fish. The complex print contains images of soldiers wearing military uniform hidden among the flowers and foliage, tapping into the universal concerns of conservation.

Print by Hussein Chalayan.

Print designed by Rory Crichton.
The subject matter, unexpected and
idiosyncratic, subverts the glamour
inherent in the fashion label Giles.

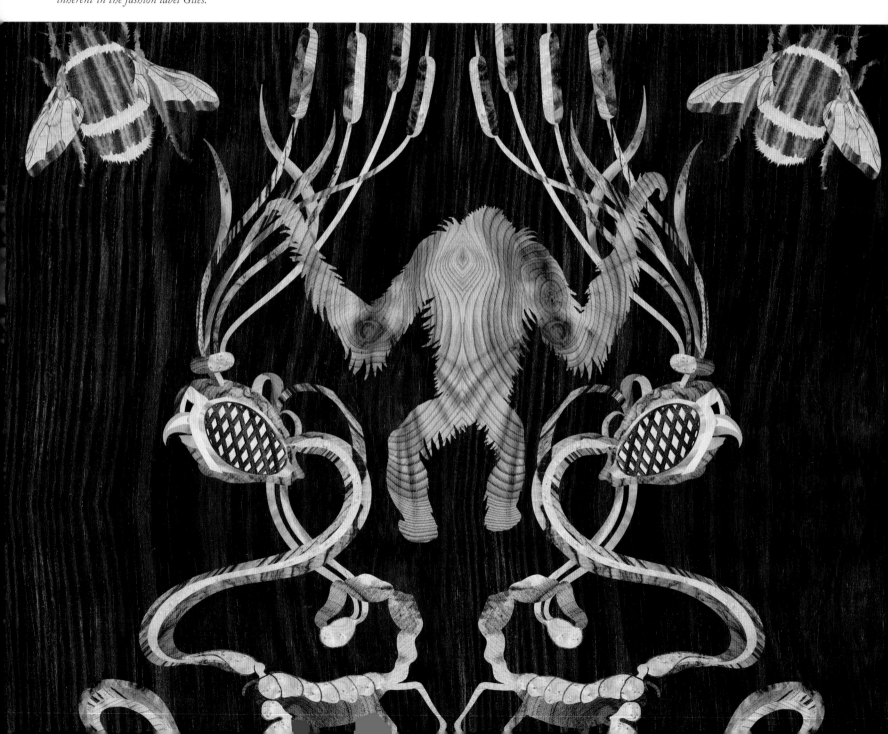

An example of a design by Rory
Crichton for Giles that is also
translated into a woven fabric for
the label by Stephen Walters &
Sons Ltd.

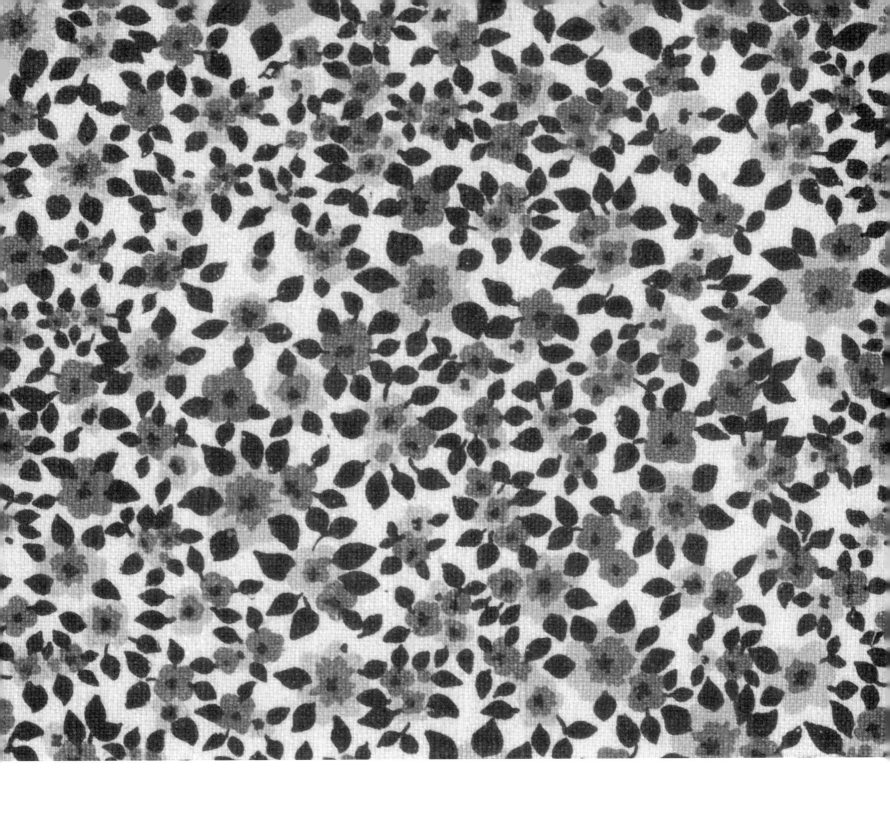

The British-born designer Ann-Louise Roswald almost invariably draws her inspiration from flowers. 'I sometimes work from an original flower painting, or just doodle. The floral motif can be very simple, but enormously effective. I like playing with marker pens. Some of our most successful designs are a single-colour print that has its origins in work I've done with a marker pen. I do a lot of experimenting. I love the process of printing and I am very drawn to it technically; printing on knitted fabrics, spraying with water to disperse the colour, experimenting with devore, making things look aged.'

Roswald is also involved in, and responsible for, all aspects of the design process, from the original print idea to the final garment. Her interpretation of nature has a crispness, clarity and freshness that owes something to her Swedish heritage on her father's side. After twice winning the New Generation Award at London

Fashion Week she knew that she was in business, and that her aesthetic could have contemporary appeal. 'The first time we showed at London Fashion Week we sold to all six of Barney's New York stores. We realized then that things had become serious.' The company has grown organically, and quickly. Her husband and business partner Nick Hartley insists that 'it is a marathon, not a sprint'. He deals with all non-product matters such as business practices, marketing and sales so that Roswald is free to concentrate on her abilities as a designer.

'I like to have full creative freedom. I love painting, and use gouache on paper or oil paints on canvas. I am a painter at heart, which is why I prefer everything to be screen-printed.' There is the sense that Roswald sees digital printing as 'unnatural', unlike the craft process of screen printing. 'I want intense colour, and you just don't get that with digital printing. With screens I love the way that where the colour

Above: *Natasha Law and Ann-Louise Roswald passing the squeegee over the specifically sited silk screen stencil to push colour through the mesh onto the fabric beneath.*

separation overlaps you get an extra colour. That way, you can build up layers of colour that lend intensity and also a vintage quality to the work. I'm definitely a "hands-on" sort of person.'

As the business has grown so have the demands on her time, though even so she still prefers to kodatrace her own screens. She values time spent doing such tasks as a time for reflection, as well as taking pleasure in the process. This artisan approach influences the direction of her work. 'I'm not interested in fashion trends, and I don't read fashion magazines. Neither do we visit trade fairs such as Premier Vision or Indigo. We exist in our own world and I go by gut instinct. It is important to have your own signature, to find what you are happy with and stick with it.'

Roswald's style is distinctive and easily recognizable. 'I love embellishment, whether it is printed, embroidered or woven, and I pay as much attention to the cut of the garment as I do to the print.' Her direct involvement extends to keeping in touch with the suppliers. 'Winter prints are more "mature", softer, more muted and textured, and we use cashmere, mesh wool, felting. I make a

Designs by Ann-Louise Roswald: the wrap dress in 'Daisy Reef' (right) and the high-waisted smock dress in 'Gerbera' printed on cotton and silk satin .

point of keeping in contact with the mills in Scotland. All the embroidery is done in China or India, and the printing in Italy, but all our final garment production is based in the UK.'

As an admirer of the 19th-century Arts and Crafts movement, and recognizing the intrinsic value of the designer being involved in manufacture, Roswald is collaborating with artist and illustrator Natasha Law. 'It can be very lonely working on your own in the studio, so it's great to participate in a joint enterprise.' The two are working together on a range of individual garments to be showcased in galleries and window displays of exclusive stores around Europe and North America. 'We are really fusing art and fashion, and we aim to make something unique, and as beautiful off the body as it is on the body. The pieces are simple wrap skirts on which we have screen printed the outline of birds that are then hand painted before being sent to India to be embellished with embroidery. The collaborative approach of the "Lou Lou and Law" line of individually crafted garments expresses the integrity of the hands-on approach in determining a unique product.'

Print designs by Ann-Louise Roswald (left and right). The texture of the cloth complements the bold, simple shapes of the flowers and the constrained colour palette.

Left: *'Large Daisy'* and *'Candy Floral'* (right) *by Ann-Louise Roswald.*
Screen-printing allows for the overlapping or overprinting of colour from the
separation process, giving a 'vintage' feel to the print.

Italian-born designer Allegra Hicks uses a less graphic and more abstract approach to sourcing from nature, giving her work intimations of the classical. Her interpretation of the organic is delicate, but sure. A key colourist, she transmutes forms into gentle, subtle prints that embellish rich, seductive fabrics such as stretch satins, crepes and chiffons. 'I'm excited because prints have come to life this season, like they were in the 60s and 70s. They are how I start every collection.' Already renowned for her designs for interior textiles, Hicks moved into fashion in 1998 with her kaftan collection, becoming the first designer to see the potential of this new summer must-have. 'No one was doing kaftans then. I didn't want big ethnic tents – ethnic is over. I wanted something that could be worn off the beach, from day to night.' The simplicity of the kaftan's shape lends itself particularly well to print. Originally a long belted tunic worn in Persia in the 16th century, it has connotations of other, more mysterious and exotic cultures. Briefly popular with the hippie counterculture in the 1960s, it has become a classic summer item, with embellishment integral to its appeal.

Allegra Hicks studied design at the Politecnico in Milan, before going on to study fine art at the Ecole Supérieure de Peinture in Brussels. This cultural heritage is reflected in her source material, she says. 'Creativity is a process of interpreting our history and the world around us. Designers are not the ultimate creators; we are result of what has gone before. Consider how the cave paintings of prehistoric man inspired painting in turn-of-the-century France. Think of the portraiture of Renaissance Italy, how can we forget that? However, you have to filter things with your own eyes. If you are in touch with your own self, then your work will have authenticity. When you are developing as a designer you think, "I wish I could have been Matisse", but then you grow out of it. At some point you have to be your own person. I spent a long time finding my pattern vocabulary, creating my own alphabet.'

She acknowledges that ideas can take time to come to fruition. 'You may see something previously and be inspired by it five years later, such as a tile you saw in Marrakesh. The mind takes time to filter memories. I always think of Proust. Why? Because it makes you feel so cosy, that particular day in that particular summer.'

Left: *Subtle, graded colour and quiet tones on the motifs represent a pared down natural form in this design by accomplished colourist Allegra Hicks.* Opposite: *Directional kaftan top and skirt by Allegra Hicks.*

'Waterlily' by Allegra Hicks, a design in three different colourways printed on luxurious fabrics such as silk georgette, silk satin and cotton voile.

Drawing is the first step of the process for Hicks. 'I draw for at least two hours every day, and then I do the first print in watercolour – I like to see that hand element. Only then do I use the computer to change the colourways.' The simplicity of the designs is upheld by the limited number of colours ('I don't like to use more than four or five screens'). Her colour palette is sophisticated, cool and classical: jade, burnt umber, Prussian blue. Garment realization comes after the long lead-time during which the prints are being finalized. 'From concept to the screen being approved is two months, and the sampling takes another month. That is the moment when you see the print come alive, and you decide how to use it. One print can be used in so many different ways. I'm interested in flow, in the way the fabric touches the body. I love to change scale and colour and make motifs travel through print, embroidery or weave.' While traditionally it may have been the designer's task to stylize plants and animals, the designer now has the opportunity to relish the authenticity of the image by reproducing it realistically. Modern technology enables the print designer to capture the impossible and freeze the moment. The flight of thrown water or the cresting of a wave can both be transferred from the camera to the cloth in one step. Textile designer Rory Crichton's butterfly print for Gucci's spring/summer 2005 menswear collection was entirely composed on the computer. 'I worked from lots of images, and put the butterfly into a very simple repeat – wing to wing, with not much background showing. The background is black, very chic. A dark background can change the way a floral design, in particular, is perceived. It creates an "edgier", more dramatic image, and takes the print one step further from being "natural".'

FLIGHTS OF FANCY

The flourish of feathers has always been used to symbolize sexual display, both in the natural world and in fashion. Peacock feathers in particular are associated with extravagant posturing; the lavishness of the colours, the iridescence of the surface, and the recurring 'eye' motif have all contributed to their mythical status, either as objects of deification or, for the superstitious, as harbingers of bad luck. Subject to popular revivals at times perceived as 'decadent', from the Aesthetic movement of the late 19th century to the Art Nouveau revival in the psychedelic 1960s, the feathers are once more a popular motif, particularly with designer Matthew Williamson. His handkerchief-point peacock print dress is seen on all the current cohort of beautiful women who buy into Williamson's elegant version of romantic bohemianism. As one of Britain's most successful independent designers, he has an acute awareness of the key ingredients that go into making an iconic dress.

Williamson first appeared on the London fashion scene in 1997 with the rainbow colours of his 'Electric Angels' collection – eleven acid-bright outfits modelled by Kate Moss, Jade Jagger and Helena Christensen. He recalls the impact of that first collection. 'I was not into all that grey, structured stuff. My clothes were the antithesis of everything that was around then. Buyers felt that they had discovered a little jewel. It's the only collection where I didn't use print. I would have done if I could, but I couldn't afford it. Print is an expensive process.'

Since then, print has been the key element of every collection. 'It's how I show my character, my personality,' he says. At the beginning of each season, Williamson and his textile specialist Ann Ceprynski discuss the concept that will provide the impetus for the new collections. 'Ann does an enormous amount of research, and then we work closely with

Belford Prints on the technical development of the print. They do our sampling and are our main suppliers. We decide whether to use digital or screen, depending on the amount of colours we want to use, and then it takes three months to tweak and make any amendments and see the strike-offs.'

Williamson confesses to a lasting obsession with colour. 'Colour has always been an integral part of my life – it's why I love what I do. I love experimenting with different combinations.' The colour palette of the label may fluctuate in its intensity, depth or fluorescence with every collection, but colour is always integral to the label.

Although a more naturalistic or subdued palette of colour may occur, such as a range of greens from eau de nil to pale turquoise, it is still deployed with a heightened sensitivity and a desire to flatter. This is also the first consideration with the print design. 'It is hard to wear a bold print – it can be consuming or

Opposite: *Exploiting the power of animal prints, Dolce and Gabbana are masters in overt sexuality as in this leopard print evening dress.* Below: *a more subtle variation, zebra stripes cut into complex shapes by Christopher Bailey for Burberry Prorsum.*

overwhelming. I'm wary of scale, and you have to be sensitive to its implications for the cut of the dress. It is dangerous to concentrate just on the print; print and cut run in tandem. They are equally important, and the designer has to keep a delicate balance between the two.'

Print ideas are usually inspired by the natural world, not only peacock feathers but also including butterflies and dragonflies. These images, which are stereotypically feminine, lend themselves to imaginative pattern cutting. 'The peacock feather is an exotic motif, but it can be used in a graphic way,' Ann Ceprynski explains. 'It is curvy and sensuous but becomes graphic by t he use of colour and placement. Highlight the colour in the "eye" and it becomes futuristic.'

Williamson's commitment in adhering to his vision of colour and print was vindicated by the opening of his London flagship store on Bruton Street in 2004. The shop incorporates every aspect of the designer's vision, the interior a reflection of his mantra. 'My approach is simple: colour, pattern, and texture.'

A WALK ON THE WILD SIDE

Vividly realistic representations of animals by our prehistoric ancestors predate any evidence of geometric design. The earliest cave paintings show human beings impersonating creatures, with hunters dressing in animal skins not only as a form of camouflage to deceive the prey, but also to take on some of the mythical qualities of the hunted beast. The people of Papua New Guinea still score their skin in imitation of the crocodile, to ensure their protection from the predator. The human ability to capture representational images was confirmed with the discovery in France, Spain and elsewhere during the 20th century of cave paintings executed more than 30,000 years ago.

Animals with markings have always been perceived as culturally suspect. 'Animals with coats either striped (*tigridus*) or spotted (*maculosus*) are creatures to fear. They can be cruel and bloodthirsty like the tiger, hyena and leopard, thieves like the trout or the magpie, sly like the snake or wasp, diabolic like the cat or the dragon. Even the zebra passes for a dangerous animal at the end of the Middle Ages. This mistrust, this fear, even, of spotted or striped animals has left an enduring mark on Western imagination.'[iv] Likewise today, the wearing of animal skins is perceived as a desire to convey the same dangerously predatory instincts as those of the big cats. Initially made popular in the West by the British desire for trophies from the colonies in the early 20th century, leopard skin has been intermittently embargoed since 1975, when the Convention on International Trade in Endangered Species (CITES) was established. Now designers have to find a way of interpreting the skin that retains the glamour of the original without compromising modern sensibilities.

The spotted coat of the female leopard, the female being the fiercest fighter, is perceived as representing the archetypal femme fatale, implying killer instincts in dealing with a potential mate. Wearing animal skin, the woman becomes both the hunter and the hunted. Hollywood confirmed the 'man eating' stereotype during the 1950s and 1960s, posing such stars as Rita Hayworth and Ava Gardner in skin-tight leopard print, implying all sorts of erotic intent. The contemporary use of animal prints is now much more subtle and deft. The print is put into a modern context; less second skin – which has connotations of the fetishistic – more tailoring; trenchcoats, trousers, constructed evening dresses.

Whether reduced to abstract form or as an exact replication of the animal's skin, animal prints have now become a constant with Italian-born Roberto Cavalli, expert designer of the dramatic occasion dress. Initially renowned for an innovatory printing process on fine-quality leather, Cavalli presented his first eponymous collection in 1970. During the 1980s he reworked leather and denim patchwork, printing over and embellishing the surface in an attempt to carve a niche in a market preoccupied with Japanese minimalism and conceptual clothes. Eva Cavalli recalls, 'Minimalism helped us – the end of minimalism gave us a new audience.'[v] The Cavallis' concentration on baroque, elaborate print designs during the 1990s projected the label into the arena of the fail-safe red-carpet statement dress beloved by celebrities.

Italian design labels are unequivocally lavish in their use of fur, a predilection that continues into copies of the real thing. Alongside Cavalli, Domenico Dolce and Stefano Gabbana, who started their design label in 1985, are renowned for their use of animal prints. Since their 1992 collection their seductive version of femininity has been influenced by Federico Fellini's cult film *La Dolce Vita* (1960). In referencing Italian film stars of the 1950s and 60s

Opposite: *a cleverly configured menagerie of deer and antelope form a figurative camouflage print outfit by Eley Kishimoto.*

such as Sophia Loren, and using models such as Isabella Rossellini and Monica Bellucci for their advertising campaigns, the clothes evidence a Mediterranean sensuality. Underwear as outerwear and sharp-suited tailoring are added to the use of animal prints to enable the designers to engage with the demand for clothes that are a confident fashion statement. They explain that 'without animal prints there would be no divas, or even divinities.'[vi]

The patterned skins of animals, which provide such optical playfulness and seductive associations to the print designer, have emerged through evolutionary pressures, causing various species – both predator and prey – to develop markings that render them inconspicuous to their predators or that dazzle their victims. The colouring of many animals varies in depth, being darker on the back and lighter underneath. This variation breaks up the surface of the animal and obscures its position – a technique copied by military defence to disguise personnel and equipment. Camouflage derives from the French word *camoufler*, meaning 'to blind or veil'. The first recorded use of the word in English was in the *London Daily News* on 25 May 1917 ('The art of hiding anything from your enemy is termed camouflage').

Camouflage was appropriated in the 1960s by anti-war protesters, who subverted its military connotations as a way of showing their defiance of the war in Vietnam. Instead of being used to allow the individual to merge into the background as intended, wearing army surplus camouflage clothing became a provocative act, as well as a utilitarian one, being cheap, hard-wearing and accessible. Although American designer Stephen Sprouse transposed his friend Andy Warhol's camouflages onto clothes in the late 1980s, it was fashion label Maharishi that really introduced 'disruptive pattern material' (DPM), a military term, into the mainstream.

Hardy Blechman, Maharishi's creative director, started recycling army surplus garments in 1996 with the introduction of the label's first fashion collection, embellishing the original fabric by overdyeing, screen printing and embroidery. He was attracted to military surplus by the styling and technical detail of the garments, but above all by the opportunity to recycle an overabundance of stock.

His concern – and continual endeavour – is to elevate DPM to a level where its military overtones become subordinate to its visual appeal, turning it into a representation of the beauty and versatility of nature, and into a force for peace.

The majority of designers have now flirted with the concept of camouflage, and the images they use are, more often than not, divorced from any military connotation – an example being Fake London's interpretation using silhouettes of mainland Britain. John Galliano is also a fan. 'As artists and designers find inspiration in the world around them, it is somewhat natural that either deliberately or subconsciously the camouflage print creeps into their line of vision and translates into their works. It is not, I believe, in any form a political or social reference of any kind, rather a creative mind's subliminal and aesthetic reaction to an everyday contemporary stimulus.

'It's the concept of the decontextualization of this print that I find interesting. As a designer I have always enjoyed the juxtaposition of the savage and the refined, it has been a constant recurring part of my work over the past 20 years. The camouflage lends itself so perfectly to the mixing of something brute with something elegant – think hard-line militia with soft, flowy chiffon ruffles. It's that streetwear vocabulary of surplus with a chic take on it. There is a certain irony in the idea of using this print, originally designed to conceal male soldiers from the enemy, for the totally opposite purpose of adorning women's bodies in the objective of enhancing their attractiveness to the opposite sex. What once belonged exclusively to a male-dominated and macho world now also belongs to the contemporary woman.'[vii]

Opposite: *Maharishi 'Bonsai Forest' camouflage cotton tussar blazer.* Overleaf: *Maharishi 'Culture DPM: British Bonsai' camouflage print. The majority of designers have at some time deployed the infinite variety in camouflage-inspired patterns for garments ranging from bikinis to eveningwear.*

Psychedelia meets nature in a design by Rory Crichton for Giles.

The relationship between humankind and nature is a potent one; no matter how urban the environment or how thrillingly complex the intensity of life in the city, there is a connection that cannot be severed. Textile designer Patricia Belford remembers a director of Savile Row tailors Gieves and Hawkes rolling on the grass outside the print factory to imprint grass stains on his shirt, for the image to be scanned and replicated on other shirts to be sold in the store. Nature is imbued with mystical overtones, from Pisanello's 15th-century *Vision of St Eustace*, which records his epiphany among the flowers and trees with animals, birds and butterflies looking on, to St Francis's spiritual accord with animals and William Shakespeare's loving evocation of woodland flowers:

> *I know a bank where the wild thyme blows,*
> *Where oxlips, and the nodding violet grows,*
> *Quite over-canopied with luscious woodbine,*
> *With sweet musk-roses, and with eglantine.*

Plants give us solace, and animals lend us their strength. However inappropriate representations of flora and fauna are on city streets and sidewalks, designers will continue to attempt to replicate that mysterious source of well being. Print has a powerful way of conveying the importance of the individual in a world of mass production.

chapter three
abstract

Abstract prints are divorced from pictorial
representation; they do not portray any kind of reality.
Unlike floral or animal prints, they are unfamiliar and
have the potential to be more demanding on the
eye. They are fractured, unreal, opposite to nature,
and this combined with the cut of the garment can
create a complex visual conundrum.

'In adorning the body an order is superimposed on an existing order, respecting or sometimes contradicting the symmetries of the organic form.'

E H Gombrich (1909–2001) [i]

There is an immediate appeal, and yet a challenge, in clothing the human body in abstract pattern. The tension lies in the fluidity of the body animating a graphic style that may be purely geometric and is certainly non-figurative. Abstract patterns are inherently oppositional to the human form, creating an ambiguity that either disguises or enhances the clothed body. Abstract pattern-making has an ancient history and is concerned with notions of repetition. Very often it has developed out of the use of identifying marks, signs or symbols, the original meaning of which it may be impossible to retrieve. Imitation of successful working processes is another explanation for early abstract patterning, based on models such as bricks built up into a wall or the interweaving of wooden latticework. Finally, there was the desire to decorate for its own sake, with the original meaning of the marks again being obscured by later developments. [ii]

Abstract art has its origins in the 19th century, when photography began to take over the basic function of representation. Abstraction in both art and design continues to preoccupy and engage designers today. The human form itself does not become a living, breathing canvas or work of art. Rather, the designer fashions an entirely new visual language without associations or precedents, and allows shapes and forms to emerge that have no counterpart in nature.

The difference between imposing a cultural artefact onto a garment, such as the Piet Mondrian painting used by Yves Saint Laurent in his 1965 collection, and the current practice of placing interacting geometrical forms on the body, is that the latter are customized to the body – and very often customized to a minute garment pattern piece.

Designers now engineer the print onto the body in a way that can only be achieved through modern technology and fabrics, and with a greater sensitivity and awareness of the human form. We have now become attuned to seeing the outlines of a figure – uncorseted, athletic – in a way unheard of when Sonia Delaunay cut her Cubist-inspired, brightly coloured canvases into the unstructured clothes of the 1920s. Then, the economy and formal simplicity of the cut of the garments made them an ideal vehicle for her printed designs.

The establishment of a fashion and textile department at the Wiener Werkstätte in Austria in 1903 was the first indication of a new abstraction in textiles for furnishings and fashion. Under the auspices of Eduard Josef Wimmer-Wisgrill, the innovatory designs of zigzags, chevrons, broken stripes and circles brought a new energy to cloth, typified by Carl Krenek's block-printed dress fabric 'Blitz', a lightning-flash stripe overlaid with flattened circles. In 1923 Varvara Stepanova also attempted to integrate print design into the garment in her Utopian fashion designs for the First State Textile Factory in Moscow. Their interlocking geometric shapes were intended to be a break from the past, denying any historical or cultural heritage.[iii] These attempts to impose abstraction on the human form were perfectly suited to the elongated, androgynous fashionable shape of the era, but animation is a prerequisite of clothes, and as cutting-edge designer Jonathan Saunders points out, 'Print must relate to the silhouette.'

When in 1963 the American dress manufacturer Larry Aldrich commissioned textile designer Julian Tomchin to base a collection on the paintings of Op artists such as Richard Anuszkiewicz and Bridget Riley, the artists were understandably displeased. When art is transposed directly into fashion, a dislocation occurs. Duplication may cheapen, rendering the object temporary and disposable, but more importantly, it denies the artist's intentions. Once the metamorphosis has occurred, as it inevitably does, from art object to design movement, fashion inevitably participates.

Abstract designs very often have connotations of the futuristic, perhaps because they appear during periods of intense artistic cultural activity. The Vorticsm of World War I, the Cubism and Futurism that influenced the Art Deco movement of the 1920s and 1930s, and the Abstract Expressionism of 1950s America; all are examples of the way in which artistic movements consistently influence design.

Far left: the simple curvy cut of this coat by Eley Kishimoto allows the swirling abstract shapes of the print full recognition.

Unravelling tubes of bright pop-art colour intersect with each other in this print design by Rory Crichton for Luella.

RENOUNCING PERSPECTIVE

Opposite (right): *The revival of interest in mid-20th-century artist-designed prints for interiors has inspired fashion designers such as Miuccia Prada in this beaded shift dress for Mui Mui.* Opposite (left): *Orla Kiely auto-hued 'Keyhole' print.*

Fashion designer Miuccia Prada uses prints inspired by the post-war aesthetic of modernity. The original artist-designed printed fabrics of that era were a dramatic contrast to what had gone before, and reflected the new-found interest in space-age technology. The designs of Barbara Brown for London interiors store Heals, and the products of manufacturers such as David Whitehead and the Edinburgh Weavers, produced designs of abstract modular shapes that informed so much of contemporary domestic design during the 1960s and 1970s. Even then, the barriers between furnishing and fashion usage were disappearing. Many home dressmakers, eager to use the much-improved sewing machines then on the market, were beguiled by the new designs for interiors and daringly created their own garments from them. The resoundingly retro motifs have now been reinterpreted for Prada's offshoot label Miu Miu; they are large in scale, repeating only once or twice on an abbreviated summer silhouette. Using large-scale patterns on voluminous garments conceals the body's parameters, instead of exposing them.

Pattern's first requirement is to hold the eye, be neither too confusing nor too boring. It is a fine balance, and one successfully navigated by Dublin-born designer Orla Kiely. 'I have always loved pattern – there is something about it that literally draws you in. The appeal is in its regularity; even if the pattern is random, it is random in a regular way.' Although there are elements of the representational in abstract designs, it is the organization of space and the graphic flatness of the motifs that give a feeling of abstract pattern, one particularly suited to the screen or rotary printing process. 'I love the instantaneous nature of screen-printing. Whatever you design on paper, it looks a million times better on fabric; you are never disappointed. The same principle applies to colour.' The colour palette is distinctive. 'I use bright colours, but include a lot of tones. The most commonly used adjective about my work is that it is fresh. There is a clarity and boldness in the repetition that makes people feel happy. There is nothing

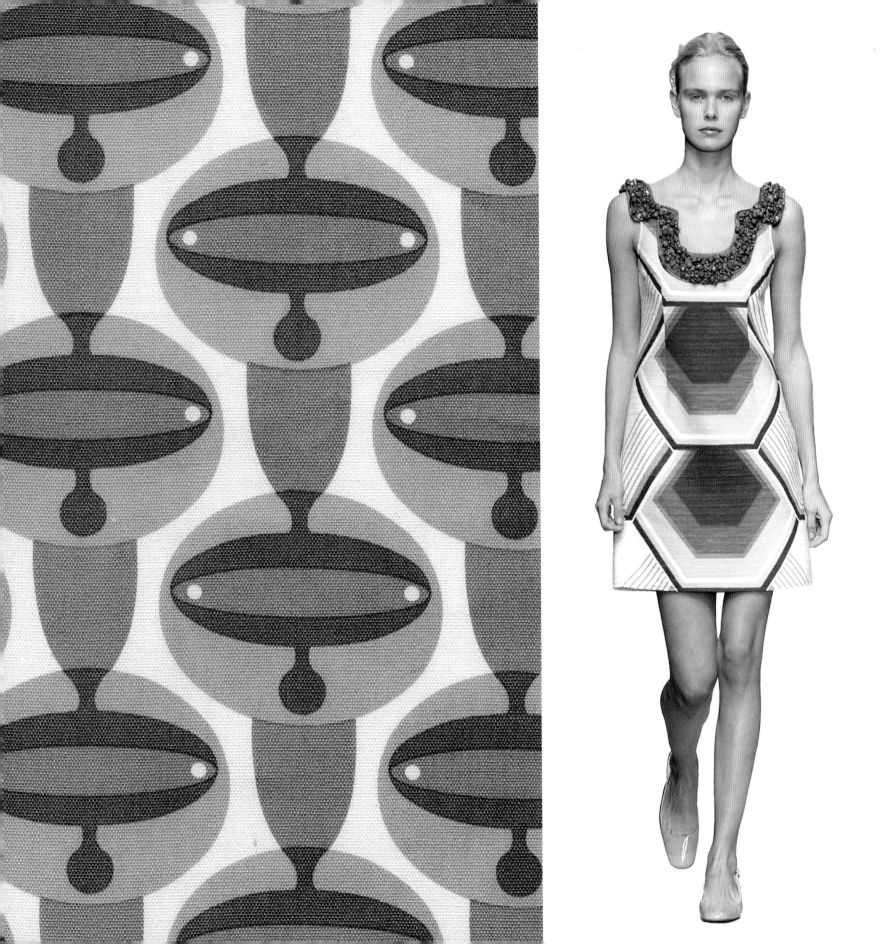

Below: *Orla Kiely extends her design practice into fashion accessories as well as providing lengths of fabric in her typically fresh designs. Bag in 'flower oval' print and fabric design in 'Modular' (right).*

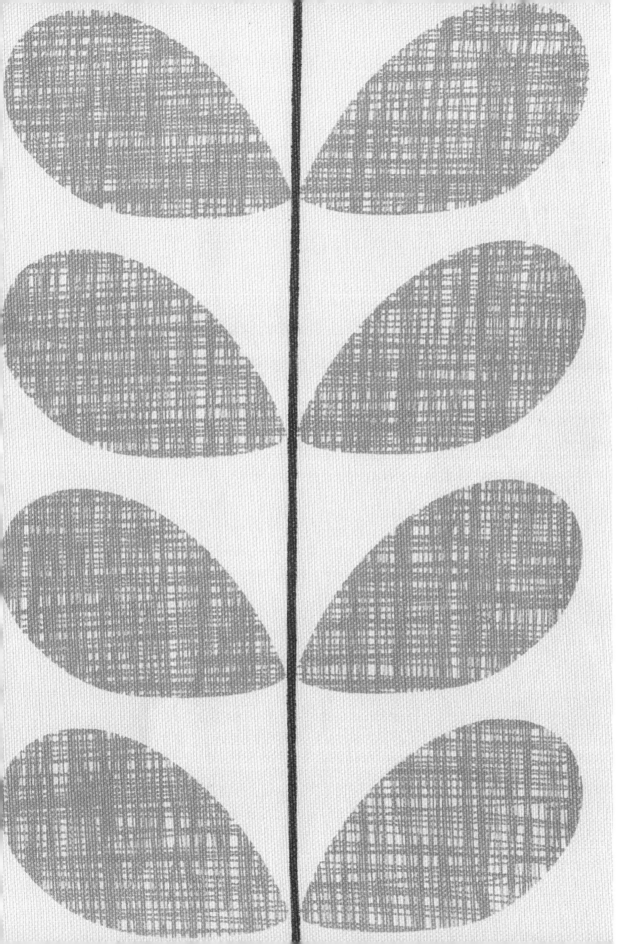

'Apples and Pears' and the 'Leaf'
print represent the simple repeats
and clarity of colour and form that
are typical of the work of Orla
Kiely.

Frenzied lines and intense,
dazzling patterning in this design
by Rory Crichton for Luella.

ambivalent or muted about my designs.' When designing for the body or for interiors, the criteria for using the print are always the same. 'If everyone in the studio loves it, I use it. Print is a way of expressing yourself, whether for the home or in fashion, and people are drawn to bold prints. Pattern always comes first, but decisions about the base cloth are important. Structure or drape will change the look of a print, and I love the contrast between the graphic and the fluid.'

When confronted with a garment describing an abstract image, the eye makes a decision to follow either the line of the body or the demanding lines of the pattern. This is particularly true of large-scale abstraction, which may take up the whole of the garment and be engineered to contour the body. Small-scale abstract pattern, by contrast, is perceived as just another surface, and so the parameters of the body remain paramount. Abstract pattern is less frequently used than the more easily recognizable floral or folkloric motifs. There is something inherently smart, in both meanings of the word, about abstract pattern: it is somehow more suitable for formal dress than any other print, and also considered in some way more 'cerebral'. Abstract pattern is used to reinforce notions of speed and performance in dress. Pattern can be used to delineate the musculature of the body by emphasizing its athleticism and imposing marks that narrow, lengthen or broaden the appearance of the body, or even distort it entirely.

An abstract pattern is, by definition, never a representation of anything specific, but is always concerned with the subject matter at one remove. Textile designer Rory Crichton, collaborating with Giles Deacon, is moving towards less representational prints. 'Last season we were getting too specific with our images of creatures. People tire of something that is immediately recognizable; we want to be chicer and smarter. Abstract prints have more longevity.'

Their collaboration is a two-way process. 'I also work for the Gucci Group and Pucci,' says Crichton, 'but they are much more prescriptive with what they want me to do. Working with Giles we can make it anything we want. We have decided to have an art class; we went out and bought some acrylic paints and we mess around, in a purely abstract way, just to mix it up.' There is greater freedom for the designer in dealing with abstraction rather than representation, by the very nature of its execution. Crichton describes the spontaneity and accidental nature of the design process: 'It's a good way of doing things; rather than filtering through PhotoShop, happy accidents happen.'

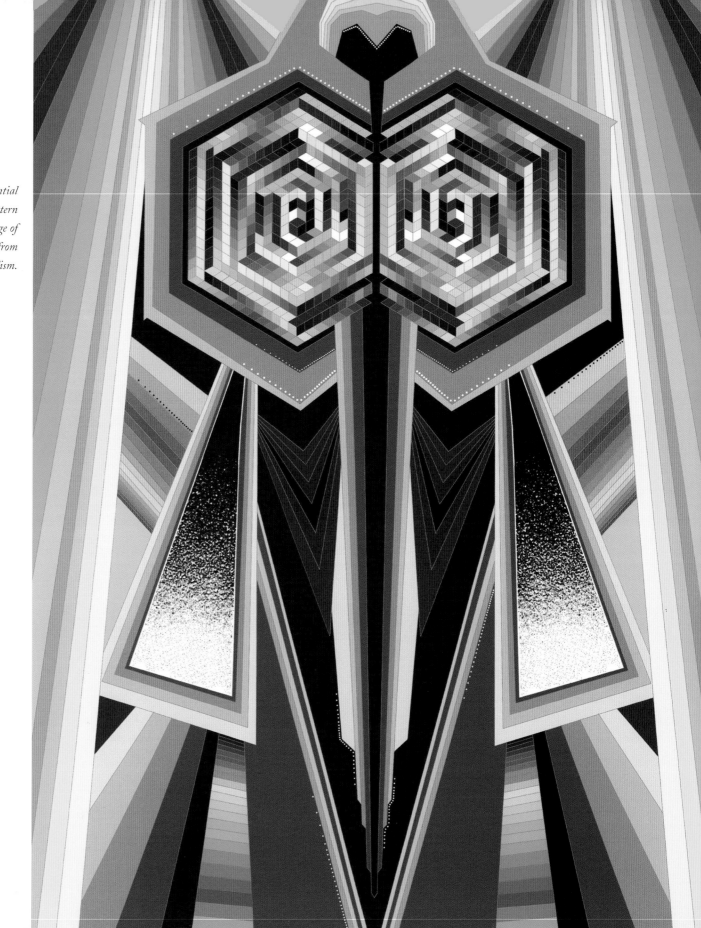

Jonathan Saunders' influential investigation of colour and pattern gave momentum to a change of direction away from 20th-century minimalism.

are working on a small scale and the acrylic painting will be scanned in and scaled right up – we will take it in and out of focus to create an illusion of depth. A photographed image of graduated tone works better on digital.' Colour is of far more significance when dealing with abstraction than with figurative prints. All designers acknowledge that a bad print design will still sell if given a good colourway, while a good design will not sell with a bad one. For non-representational images, this is even more true. Rory Crichton also acts as a colour consultant for the Gucci Group, so he is well placed to exploit its qualities, changing the amount of colour saturation if necessary when the design is initially sampled at the Centre for Advanced Textiles at the Glasgow School of Art.

APPLYING GEOMETRY

Oskar Schlemmer was a proponent of using geometry to change the shape of the human body. He was an artist and designer with the Bauhaus, the German academy founded in 1919 by the architect Walter Gropius to unify all aspects of art and design. Schlemmer's series of sketches, entitled 'Means of Transforming the Human Body by Use of Costume', which he created during the costume-design process for the stage work *Triadic Ballet* (1922), is one of the central inspirations in the work of the Scottish-born designer Jonathan Saunders.

Saunders is renowned for his kaleidoscopic shards and fragments of colour that dazzle the eye and define the body. Initially opting to study product design at the Glasgow School of Art, he switched to textiles in a desire to pursue a subject where the primary concern is aesthetic rather than functional. He went on to study for a postgraduate degree in print for fashion at Central St Martins School of Art in London, achieving immediate

The front and back of a garment by Jonathan Saunders blocked out as a blueprint of pattern pieces to resolve the placement of colour relationships.

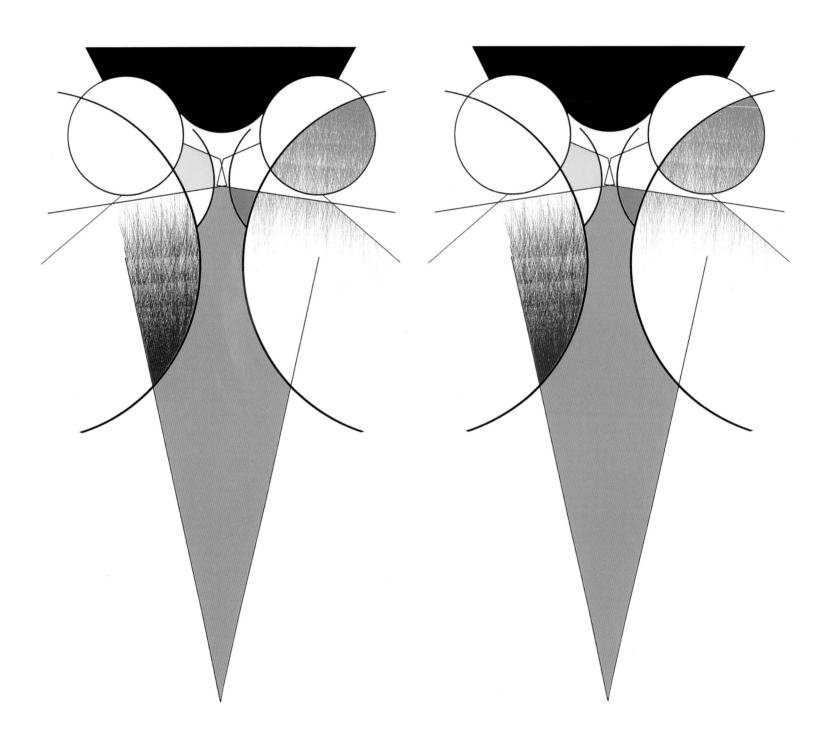

recognition on graduation when he collaborated with Alexander McQueen on a 'bird of paradise' feather print for the designer's spring/summer 2003 collection. His ability to integrate pattern into three-dimensional form, and his convincing confidence with colour, made him an ideal consultant for Italian fashion house Pucci.

Opposite: *Jonathan Saunders deploys principles of Euclidion geometry to draft his print constructions.*

Saunders's work is the antithesis of the whimsical, figurative, very often narrative prints that sometimes seem to bear little relation to the garments on which they appear. 'I'm not interested in "conversational" prints, or symbolism of any kind. My work is deliberately divorced from any kind of representation. I'm concerned with balance and line. Print for me is not just about decoration – it is much more cerebral than that. My clothes aren't about titillated decoration added on as an extra. I have an innate desire to decorate the body, very much in the way of tattooing or body painting. I like to frame the body.'

Working with the complex inheritance of such diverse artists as M C Escher, Victor Vasarély, Richard Hamilton and Jackson Pollock, Saunders's subject matter remains unequivocally abstract. The designer develops his garment and print designs simultaneously, engineering the print to fit each pattern piece using traditional craft techniques. 'Certain things you can only do by hand; I like to keep a fine art quality to my work. I hand-draw the design, and everything has to be drawn full size. I colour the outlines with a black pen, which must be closed off to enable colour separation on the computer. I then scan the print on PhotoShop A1 size, cut the pattern and screen-print the samples. There might be seventeen pattern pieces to a garment, each one with an engineered print on it of several colours, so they have to be done digitally. However, the artwork is the same, whether for screen or digital printing.'

His work is remarkable for its complex and subjective palette, in which colour is always the first consideration. 'It starts off being calculated, and then becomes uncontrollable. I think proportion is more relevant than the colour itself. Something like a tiny black line on the hem of a white dress can be utterly effective.' His virtuosity with colour includes an understanding of tone. 'Gradation of a pencil line or some crosshatching includes tonal change. Three colour prints in three colourways equals nine ways of using tone.'

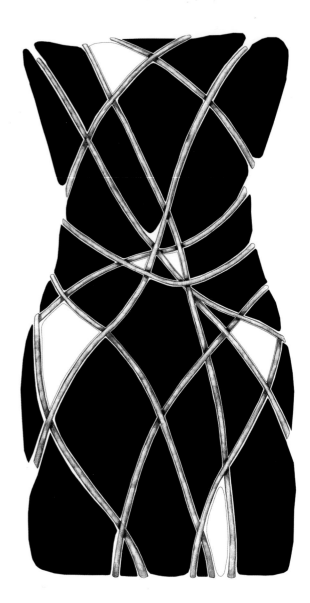

Mapping the body with a matrix of intersecting curves, Jonathan Saunders subtly evokes the bound figure. Opposite: *Pursuing abstraction and creating patterns of kaleidoscopic colour, Saunders creates engineered prints that are tailored to fit the garment (here the front and back of a dress).*

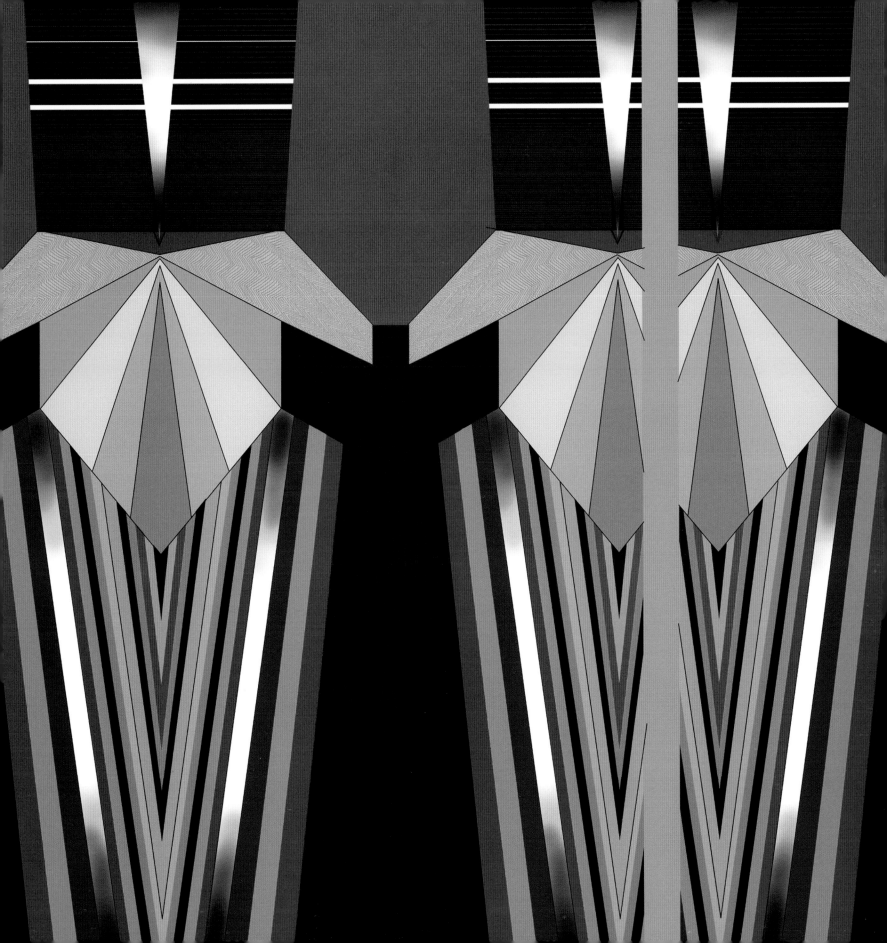

BALANCE AND FORM

According to British designer Neisha Crosland the underlying principles of textile design remain the same, whether the cloth is being made for fashion or interiors (she includes both in her practice). 'Textiles are designed and printed on the flat, but they have flexible contours. The whole point of textiles is that they become three-dimensional, whether they are on the body or on a sofa or a pair of curtains. There are the same preoccupations. Where will the motif be placed on the body? What will happen to the pattern when it turns around the corner on the sofa? Working it out is completely satisfying. The proportion, scale and play of the repeat is like the rhythm in music. Pattern can be chaotic, but it should be calming: that is the challenge.' There are some differences, however. 'Fabrics for interiors have a longer shelf life than those for fashion. The Neisha interior label is more sophisticated than the Ginka fashion label, which is lighter and more fun. With fashion you have to think of all the fabrics working together. I'm not shopping for cloth; it is very time-consuming putting together prints of differing scales, proportion and colour.'

Cloth and its properties consume Crosland. She is considered by Fleet Bigwood to be 'the most sophisticated designer around. In years to come she will be the one

Above: *A display wall in the 'Ginka' range at the Neisha Crosland fashion studio, showing work in progress and the co-ordination of designs in terms of scale, texture and colour.*
Opposite: *a montage of the many different colourways of the 'Beano!' design, all painted by hand in gouache.*

Cutting the garment patterns for the 'Ginka' range in the studio. Opposite: 'Pop!' by Neisha Crosland printed in crisp cotton poplin, stretch silk satin and also woven as a slightly quilted metallic weave.

remembered for doing brilliant things.' Her print designs utilize innovative techniques and finishes, the result of a flourishing relationship with textile designer Patricia Belford based on a mutual exchange of ideas and processes. 'I will show Neisha a technique such as selectively shrinking areas of the cloth,' Belford says, 'and then she thinks about how she can exploit it and we take it from there.' The Ginka fashion label was initially a small collection comprising sarongs, halternecks and T-shirts, and has now been extended, in response to demand, into a full ready-to-wear range. 'I didn't like leaving the design on the drawing table, and once you have started a range it has its own momentum.'

Originally, Crosland wanted to be a painter. 'I was overwhelmed when I went to an exhibition of the Russian Expressionists. It was way ahead of Picasso. I thought "how can I contribute anything new, I have nothing more to say".' A compromise seemed to be achieved by enrolling on a graphics course at Camberwell College of Art in south London. It was during the course that on a college visit to the Victoria and Albert Museum in search of the William Morris Room she got lost

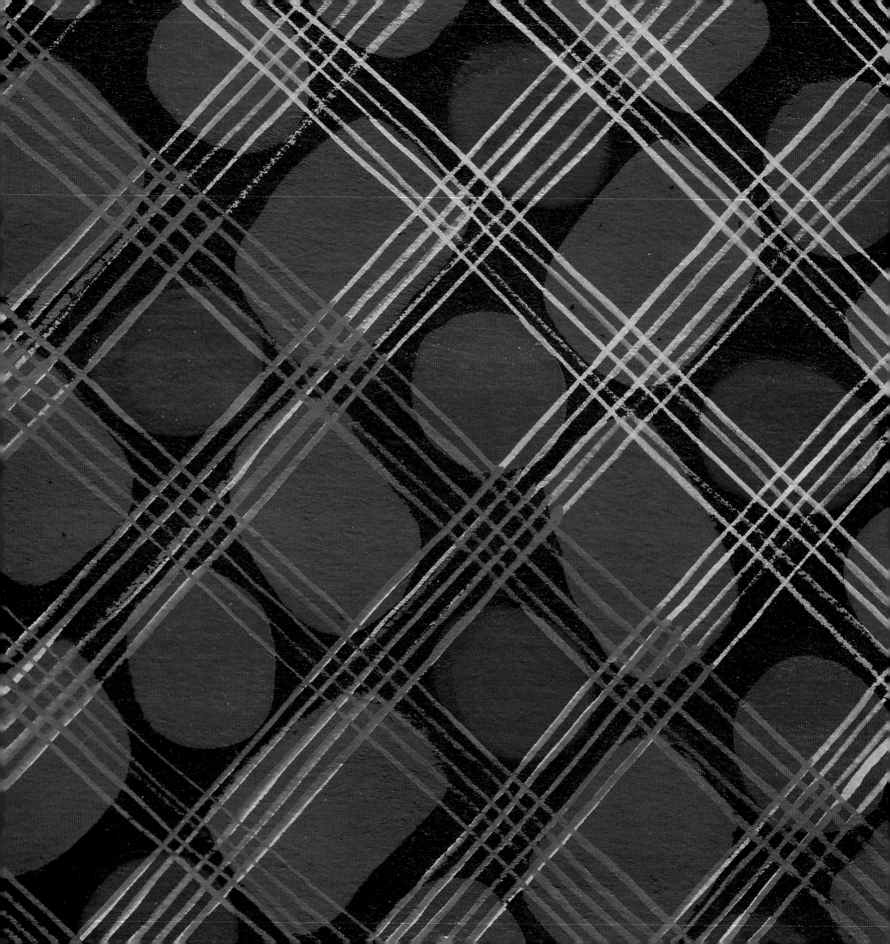

in the textile gallery and experienced something of an epiphany. 'I came across the samples of textiles from the 16th-century Ottoman Empire. They were really modern and bold and stark but also had texture; brocades and embroidery. I knew then that I needed to do textiles.' Crosland worked for the wallpaper company Osborne & Little after studying for a postgraduate degree at the Royal College of Art, and after spending some time in California she put together a portfolio. During the early 1990s Crosland's first successful design – a zebra print in velvet devoré – was produced, and is still selling.

Whether her prints are for interiors or fashion, the design process invariably starts with hand-drawn artwork. 'Designing on a computer is like eating a Pot Noodle instead of cooking real food. I am constantly drawing and painting. I use gouache and even love the smell of the paint.' Unusually, her colourways are worked out off-screen too. 'You can change the mood of a pattern by changing the colour – from neon to sober, for instance.'

However, although Crosland admits to being computer illiterate, she is excited about the possibilities of digital printing. 'Ideas and techniques come together. If it's the appropriate technique for the idea, and it's on an interesting base cloth and utilizes all

Source board in the Neisha Crosland studio. Opposite: *a close up of 'Beano!' to be printed on cotton jersey T-shirts.*

'Splat!' by Neisha Crosland, hand painted in gouache to be printed on stretch silk satin and transfer printed onto T-shirts for the 'Ginka' fashion range.

Opposite: *Liberating colour and pattern from form in this free floating design by Eley Kishimoto.*

sorts of finishes, digital printing can be the right choice.' She finds the process of abstracting pattern to be intellectually stimulating. 'Whenever journalists ask me if I am glad to see that the trend for minimalism is over I reply that my designs are minimalist. I strip the design to its bare essentials and get rid of the bits and pieces so that there are no distractions. I abstract the bare bones.'

She likens herself to a 19th-century scientist, combining the notion of aesthetic and scientific enquiry. 'I feel like a biologist: I research and classify. At the moment I am completely absorbed by the drawings of Ernst Haeckel in his 1862 book *Radiolaria*. I'm playing with the idea of the spoke. It's so versatile, and I'm incorporating an ombré quality, where the colour is graduated from light to dark.' This cerebral approach in responding to the challenge of utilizing motifs means that Crosland's work has absolute integrity. The pattern does not merely sit on the surface; it is contextualized into the cloth in a way that is particular to her label.

The pure abstraction of Saunders's work is something of a rarity in contemporary textile design: a designer more usually operates by referencing and acknowledging some sort of source. Other designers such as Crosland identify the inherent structure of their subject, producing non-representational images that are nevertheless precisely observed and analyzed, and that also explain and define the form. Design label Eley Kishimoto, for its part, combines abstraction with figurative sources. Mark Eley explains: 'When we met, Wakako's aesthetic was different from mine. She was more interested in kitsch, whereas I was more conceptual and mathematical. Now we don't need to differentiate between the two. We don't really think about what we are doing, we just do it.'

Mark Eley and Wakako Kishimoto, based in London, became a singular presence on the city's fashion scene when they started the label Eley Kishimoto in 1992. Their distinctive and conspicuous combination of colour and pattern is seen as instigating the current print revival, and continues to sell successfully in all the fashion capitals of the world. Wakako Kishimoto left Japan in 1986 to study at Central St Martins School of Art, where she gained an MA in Fashion and Print. She met her future husband, Welsh-born Mark Eley, in New York while on work placement. There has not been such a significant partnership between print and fashion since Ossie Clark and Celia Birtwell's perfect synthesis of garment and print in the late 1960s and early 1970s.

'Avant-garde designers saw print as a retro step,' explains Kishimoto. 'This started to change in the 1980s when print became integrated into catwalk collections, but it was never the main focus, only an element of the whole look. Fundamentally, that's why we started our own label.'

Consultants to some of the biggest names in fashion, including Hussein Chalayan, Jill Sander, Yves Saint Laurent, Alexander McQueen, Louis Vuitton and Marc Jacobs, Eley Kishimoto design original and iconoclastic prints in the context of a traditional craft environment. Kishimoto does not use the computer at all. 'The technical aspect of printing can be seen as a bit of a barrier, but actually any image can be produced as a print, even a doodle. I just scribble something and print it. I like the purity of the handcrafted process. It gives me time to think of other things. It is part of the rhythm of working and creates a mental space. The computer is not sophisticated enough yet. I have never seen a great digital print. What is the point of putting a photograph on a dress?'

Kishimoto is careful to explain that the garment is not subservient to the print. 'We don't think of the print first, and then design the garment. As much consideration goes into our pattern cutting as it does to the print.' Eley concurs: 'Most designers don't know how to use an all-over print, but we enjoy it.'

The business is based in a former jam-packing factory in Brixton, south London, and has the ad hoc atmosphere of a truly creative environment. There is ample evidence in the studio of Mark's ability to create workable solutions to the demands of running a thriving enterprise. Still in use is the home-made screen-print exposure unit he built from a couple of strip lights, a sheet of glass, some tinfoil and 50 phone books dating from 1992, the year the

Eley Kishimoto's iconic 'Flash' design. The scale and repeat of this energetic abstraction renders it uniquely versatile for application in both interiors and fashion (see also overleaf).

Abstract

couple first started their professional partnership. He also designed and made the device that suspends the fabric over the print table while it is drying.

'The 3-metre print table was the first investment,' Eley recalls. 'We had no facilities for dyeing, so we printed on white cotton, as it was cheap and easy to handle. We had to steam the fabrics in buckets. For the same reason our colour palette is deliberately limited – simple primaries. The first print was royal blue and red. We had only 10 to 15 screens, so we were only able to produce four or five prints.'

Although all fabrics and garments are made under licence in Italy, the sampling is done in the studio with help from graduates of Central St Martins School of Art. They have sustained a relationship with Natalie Gibson, who is a tutor at the college, and this is typical of their ability to nourish professional relationships. Mark Eley explains: 'The way we work is an extension of the way we live. We think creativity is relative to the way we think about friendship, family, and work colleagues. We try to communicate a philosophy, not just about work, but also in our design and manufacturing relationships. Our product is an intimate expression of our creativity.'

Their iconic 'Flash' design, based on animal prints and with a repeat pattern of only 20 square centimetres, was their first design to travel across products and seasons, appearing on varied surfaces from dresses to wallpaper, and becoming a classic. The design empire of Eley Kishimoto now includes shoes, luggage, umbrellas, and furniture.

At a perceptual level abstract print on a garment confounds our expectations; as the eye travels over the body it experiences disruptions in the natural order. The designer colludes with the wearer in demanding attention. It is the movement of the body combined with the movement inherent in the print that provides such a striking visual display. There is a purity of vision in the utilization of geometric progression and the infinite permutations of geometrical form, a rigour in the rejection of the banal, and a discipline in the pursuit of the relationship between points, lines, surfaces and solids, that will always represent an achievement to the print designer.

'Birdy Bird' and 'Marbles'
by Eley Kishimoto.

chapter four
folklore, fantasy and fable

Western fashion has always appropriated and reassembled elements of other cultures, borrowing decorative details and handcrafted techniques to use as design inspiration. This can be seen as a safe way of experiencing a different kind of life, one that is free-spirited and somehow both exotic and yet more authentic, and rooted in the myths of folklore.

'The origin and development of the decoration of any nation are inseparably bound up with its history, its migrations and its commerce.'

A H Christie *Traditional Methods of Pattern Designing* [i]

Other cultures are often perceived as having nobler traditions than our own, as is the past of our own culture. As historian Eric Hobsbawm has pointed out, 'the folk' are an idealized, preindustrial peasantry, representing uncorrupted virtues, a simple way of life, and a belief in the importance of age-old traditions.[ii] In retrieving these myths, the designer relishes the accoutrements of those who have little access to Western values. Gypsies, the nomad, the Native American, the Peruvian peasant – all are grist to the designer's mill. 'Folk' dress is tied up with notions of celebration and festivities and is to do with tradition not novelty, instinct not intellect. One of the first attempts to explore the concept of 'folk' dress in the 20th century was instigated by the couturier Paul Poiret. He set up the Atelier Martine in 1911 after seeing the printed textiles of the Wiener Werkstätte on a trip to Vienna. He employed a group of young women lacking in any formal art education and encouraged them to draw from life, visiting the botanical gardens and the flower and vegetable markets.[iii] The simplified, bold floral patterns in strikingly vivid colours were to influence design for the following two decades.

The concept of 'folk', and the desirability of the naive, are directly opposed to the concept of couture. One implies handmade, rustic and homespun; the other, handcrafted, alert to change, and sophisticated. Costume, unlike fashion, remains unchanged in a changing world. There is an irony in the Western designer plundering fragments of other cultures and transforming them into expensive couture, because he or she is thereby making what was formerly unchanging into something fashionable, and therefore temporary and disposable. The world and its indigenous peoples become one massive source book, with a budget for travel built into the designer's costs. Parisian couturiers John Galliano and Jean-Paul Gaultier are both renowned for finding inspiration from all over the globe and bringing together disparate sources to create pattern on pattern. A single dress can combine embellishment and styling details that owe their origins to China, Peru and the

Design inspired by the colours and textures of Mexican artist Frida Kahlo, produced by Alexander Henry Fabrics in various colourways (see also previous page).

103

A discharge print on crepe de chine by the Furphy-Simpson Studio. A contemporary version of the paisley design, animated by the interplay of floral patterning against the plain background.

Russian Steppes. The incorporation of printed imagery into knitted, woven and embroidered cloth produces a kaleidoscope of multi-layered colour and texture, reflecting the itineraries of the designers and their teams. Visual diaries of their travels comprised such ephemera as food wrappers, travel tickets, ornaments, jewellery, market finds, threads and fabrics, as well as photographs. As John Galliano says, 'When we travel, we don't just do the tourist things. We go on to the streets to sample the local spirit. That is where we get into the nooks and crannies, where it all happens.'[iv]

Decoration may be perceived in modernist terms as anti-design, and viewed in opposition to the Bauhaus principle that form follows function and that decoration is therefore both unnecessary and irrelevant, even in some way self-indulgent and thus morally dubious. Notions of class, craft and taste are also part of the eternal tension between the romantic and the classic. The decorative process might be considered by some to come from the heart rather than the head, and even to retain elements of the spiritual. The folk dress of other countries can be understood, appreciated, and elements of it deployed without the designer necessarily going to the location. The look will be interpreted in such a way as to reinforce the signature handwriting of the label while still conveying the qualities of the idiomatic motifs. The irregular and uneven appearance of handcrafted pattern may even be reproduced in all its imperfections by modern manufacturing so as to give the appearance of being handmade, thus compromising the integrity of the original.

The identification with other cultures may not be limited to a fascination with their use of colour and pattern. Taking inspiration from these decorative traditions allows for the possibility of transposing not only the imagery but also the values of these other cultures. Embellishment of the cloth is not to do with commercial value or status but undertaken as a communal activity, to fulfil ceremonial or familial requirements, and with the simple pleasure in the activity of craft. Motifs may be highly symbolic, perhaps concerned with providing protection from evil spirits or generating an abundant harvest. While the origin of symbols such as the tree of life and the furled palm leaf remains obscure, their attraction is universal. One such motif is that of the paisley, among the most enduring inspirations for textile designers. As with the peacock feather, it is an image particularly persuasive in implying a certain romantic bohemianism and laid-back hippie chic. Sometimes thought to be the mark made by curling the hand into a fist and printing with the

little finger downwards into the cloth, the motif of the comma-shaped cone can also be thought of as a seedpod and as such a symbol of life and fertility. The pattern originated in the woven shawls of Kashmir, from the northwest of India at the edge of the Himalaya. Imported into Britain at the end of the 17th century, demand exceeded supply, and attempts were made to copy the design by weavers in the Scottish town of Paisley. This woven version proved too expensive, and cheaper, printed versions flooded the market. Designers over the ages have exaggerated and distorted the basic scroll-shaped unit, varying the length of the 'fruit' and the 'stalk' and introducing extraordinary colourways to make it their own. It has become the signature motif of Italian fashion label Etro since they first used it in 1981.

One of the earliest forms of the application of pattern to the human form is tattooing. In striving to make the body look unlike itself we distort and pervert nature by using marks that might indicate social status or replicate wounds from battle, but more often than not are images enjoyed purely for their decorative qualities. Printmaking is an extension of this natural instinct. Basic printing techniques, and the use of dyes, were first applied directly onto the human body; it was a natural evolution to transfer the innate pleasure in decoration to the medium of dress. As E. H. Gombrich writes in *The Sense of Order*, 'Decoration is part of evolution, a gradual process of mimesis, repetition, fusion and adaptation.'[v]

A screen-printed replication of the batik method of resist dyeing, utilising naive motifs in this folkloric print by Alexander Henry Fabrics.

THE ORIGINS OF PATTERN

From the Latin *pator* (via 'patron') the word 'pattern' originally meant 'parent form', and a defining characteristic of pattern is repetition using a mechanical aid such as a stencil or a block. Non-European cultures such as those of India, Africa and Japan have traditionally printed fabrics using the immediacy of block or resist methods, unchanged for centuries. Colour is applied directly to the block, which is then used to stamp the image on the cloth, either by hand or with a wooden mallet. The oldest surviving block-printed textile is a child's tunic dating from the 4th century AD. It was discovered and documented in the 19th century during excavation of the burial field of Achmim in Upper Egypt by Robert Forrer, together with an actual printing block of the same period.[vi]

In the resist method, the image is printed with a wax or starch and the fabric is dipped into dye. The printed areas resist the dye and remain white. Techniques such as tie-dyeing, the mud-resist dyed cloth of Mali, batik, and the shibori, an ancient Japanese 'shaped resist' method of stitched and bound cloth that is then dip-dyed, are all still utilized today. Miuccia Prada employed both in her spring/summer 2004 collection, and Stella McCartney featured batik – a Javanese process that means 'marking with dots' – in her spring/summer 2005 collection. Those designers who take advantage of

A collection of printed fabrics expressly made for African consumption in Manchester by the Brunschweiler factory, now called 'Tootal Batik'. At the end of the 19th century, tribal leaders would send their designs to Britain for reproduction. Initially, roller printing – and now screen printing – was used to simulate the batik process of applying hot wax with a 'tjanting' tool.

Eley Kishimoto's 'Local' collection.
A fusion of Brixton street culture
with controlled reference to
African-inspired motifs.

the traditional skills of other countries must inevitably combine them with a Western sensibility in the design element if they are to appeal to a fashion-led audience, rather than to textile collectors in search of authenticity. Jenny Hoon, who worked as project design manager on a number of development projects in India, Nepal, Zimbabwe and South Africa, acknowledges that 'the [indigenous] printers have an innate sense of spatial application. My task was to translate the print designs from being single motifs into an all-over repeat. I worked out a system using chalked lines and string to register the repeat, thinking that the printers would have to be taught the way Western art students are taught. However, they understood immediately the principles of all types of repeat, and we were able to print 50-metre bolts of cloth. In Nepal there were always block makers in the local markets to make up blocks to specific designs.' However, she also admits that it is difficult, and not necessarily desirable, to impose Western aesthetics on non-European cultures, even in the name of trade.

Inspiration is found while travelling, as the designer's luggage labels show, but a culture can also inspire when mediated through the work of a photographer, an exhibition, a dance movement, or even a locality. Eley Kishimoto's show for summer 2005 was influenced by the images seen in and around Brixton, the south London location of their studio. The experience is not ethnographic, but rather is concerned with surface, mood and interpretation. Such is the continued popularity of non-Western cultures as a source of inspiration in dress that the American designer Zac Posen coined the term 'tribalite' for a woman wearing dress associated with non-Western ethnic groups. 'It's a noun we invented to describe the "tribal socialite", a woman who understands both society and ethnicity and fused the two to invent her own philosophy and community.'[vii]

111

ARTISANSHIP REINVENTED

The apotheosis of handblock-printed fabrics was reached in Indian textiles up to the early 19th century. No other country has had such a longstanding influence on the printed cloths of other nations.[viii] An extensive trade in printed and painted cottons between India, China, Java and the Philippines predated the first arrival of Europeans via the sea route around the Cape of Good Hope in 1498. During the 20th century the establishment of European factory-style printing processes eroded the substantial skills of textile printers, including a vast knowledge of indigenous dyestuffs, but there are fashion labels that prefer to utilize the traditional craft processes rather than take advantage of the cheaper industrialized methods now available.

Australian-born designer Megan Park reveres the highly specialized talents that she uses in producing her fashion ranges. Martin Raymond believes that one of the reasons for the print revival is the application to detail that is only achievable by using traditional crafts. 'Artisanship is being reinvented. There is an interest in the beauty of detail; textiles are being produced now that would once have been relegated to museums.' Megan Park produces garments of exquisite sensibility, yet it is for the techniques, rather than the design inspiration, that she spends three months of every year with artisans in Delhi.

'If I don't go to India and oversee everything, things get lost in translation. I will have the designs sketched up in advance and have a general idea of what I would like to create, but this evolves and changes once I'm working side by side with the artisans.' The nature of the design influences her decision to use either screen or block-printing methods. 'When using wood blocks the print design usually has a particular rustic quality that I would like to emphasize. I will give the paper design to the woodcarver to be traced onto the block of wood before he carves into it. The design can be multi-coloured and as large and complicated as I like. It is vital, however, that the more complicated the design, the more precise the carving must be in order for the design to match in the repeat. Block printing will never be perfectly aligned and this lends to it a certain beauty. The small imperfections show that the design has been done by hand. This process is full of surprises and the end result is always different from the original concept.'

Opposite and overleaf: Megan Park's block-printed simple motifs and engaging play on scale are enriched by hand-embellishments.

The blocks for Park's designs are then applied to the fabric manually, relying on the trained hand of the printer to keep up a steady, seamless pattern. The dyes are

Printed and decorated fabrics from head to foot, including accessories, by Megan Park.

produced by one man who mixes the colour from memory, rather than scientific notes, the inevitable slight variations helping to ensure that the colour of each garment is unique. 'Print plays a vital part in my collection. I usually source prints through old textile design books, or perhaps I will discover something in a flea market or vintage store or with textile dealers. I am usually captured by the spirit of the print, and this evokes the essence of the collection. I will then re-work, re-scale, and re-size the print in order to modify it and make it my own.' The printed fabrics are then embellished further. 'The layering of pattern is important to me; it is essential to the look. Print is the background, and from that I can take the design in new or conflicting directions with beading and embroidery. I use Japanese glass beads, which are stitched on individually, and then two types of hand embroidery are used. The garment is even assembled using a hand-operated sewing machine.'

Megan Park completed a fashion degree before working as a textile designer in Melbourne. In 1995 she moved to London, working for Givenchy, Dries van Noten and Kenzo before finally launching her own label 1999. The response to the label varies. 'My collection can be worn by edgy fashionistas or women looking for clothes that are easy and comfortable to wear, as they are not restrictive or tight. I can't imagine doing anything graphic or hard-edged. My British customer tends to have a boho look; they wear individual pieces with other things. In America the label is bought by what my agent calls the "soccer mum" – women who buy the whole look and wear it when they want to dress casually, and they buy the whole outfit. Asia likes the accessories.

'I like to think that something bought now can be worn in ten years' time. My clothes are not a statement

for a season, though we sometimes coincide with what's happening in fashion. Women have become more experimental and less dictated to by trends, and the Megan Park label reinforces that philosophy.'

Another label that always espouses an eclectic approach, disregarding the imperative of mainstream fashion trends, is Marni. Founded in 1994 by the Castiglioni family, the label, designed by Consuelo Castiglioni, has a determined grasp of the balance between artisan and sophisticated elements. The garments incorporate appliqué, print and texture allied to a feel for proportion and cut that transcends seasonal interruptions and is enormously influential. The designer acknowledges the importance of print to the label. 'I am always, and at every moment, attracted by beautiful prints; they are, together with natural materials and colour, a bit of a trademark for me. At the beginning, it's always a fabric or a print which stimulates my creativity. Then I start mixing and matching and I decide what the silhouettes will look like. The modern touch is given by the details on which I really concentrate. They have to be sophisticated, feminine, sexy and original.'

Castiglioni has a singular vision in which the narrative of the clothes is important. 'I see my collections as precious mosaics. Assembling, bringing together different times, places, attitudes. Combining patterns, colours, fullness, and lengths. It's dressing with fragments, shreds; being a tinker of style. It is conceiving a narrative wardrobe. My aim is to satisfy a woman's natural desire for uniqueness and distinction.'

One of these distinctive qualities of the label is the characteristic Marni colour palette. 'I like combining colours and prints which normally might be considered a little eccentric, unconventional. My approach to colour is very instinctive. I have always been attracted by original colour combinations. Everything originates from a feeling, a special sensibility, something that attracts my attention. I use anything that inspires me, it can be a scrap of wallpaper, a photograph, a painting. I rarely use Pantone palettes –

I like working directly with fabrics. Textures don't all behave in the same way. One type might work in one colour, but not in others.'

This instinct to interpret non-Western culture with integrity is endorsed by the Belgian-born designer Dries Van Noten. Unusual in so cerebral a designer are his powerful and abandoned use of colour and his evident passion for pattern. His clothes are the very antithesis of minimalism. Many and various print techniques may be incorporated in a single, multi-layered garment that will become a wardrobe classic, irrespective of fashion trends. Recently celebrating his 50th collection, he emerged in the 1980s as one of the cutting edge 'Antwerp Six' – a group that also included Martin Margiela and Ann Demeulemeester – who graduated from the Antwerp Fashion Academy. His ability to transmute folkloric decoration into a modern aesthetic has always been a feature of his work; that it now coincides with fashion's preoccupation with the romantic and the bohemian was once a cause for concern. 'In the last few years I have tried to concentrate on things that are beautiful. Previously, I worried whether designs were fashionable enough or whether the press would like them. Now I create my own standards. It is scary that my work now fits fashion's mood, because that will pass – fashion goes in waves. Having worked 20 years in the business, I've known high days and hard days. Now I've learned not to panic.'[ix]

For more than a decade the label Clements Ribeiro has signified elegant decoration. Brazilian-born Inácio Ribeiro and his wife and partner Suzanne Clements were among the first of the new wave to incorporate notions of print into mainstream fashion, and have sustained a look that encompasses diverse print techniques and global references. 'When we launched our label in 1993 there was still very little going on in London, there were only 16 shows, so we couldn't help but get noticed. When we started, Prada was the cult label; minimalism had gone mainstream, which left a gap at the top end of the market for pattern, colour, decoration and

Dries Van Noten manages the interplay of prints of varied scale and colour by the punctuation of strong plain colours and textures. Opposite: Marni tulip-shaped skirt and high-waisted jacket forcefully combining garments of conflicting prints.

print. We were everything you wanted but couldn't find. We were against deconstruction, minimalism, rough edges and rawness. Our roots are in couture, we like expensive cloth and finishing.' The controlled folkloric patterning allied to well-crafted elegance epitomizes the Clements Ribeiro style, and attracted the Paris fashion house Cacharel. 'Fashion is all about luxury, and we felt it would be a challenge; we saw it as a prize.' With their intervention Cacharel is now once again a coveted label. 'We didn't want a retro feel. Cacharel had no archives, and we wanted to capture an essential youthfulness and freshness, using a contemporary language.'

IMAGES AND ARCHETYPES

It is mythical countries and legendary people and places that Brazilian-born Bruno Basso and Englishman Christopher Brooke describe with their luscious colour and swirling lines. It takes a while for the eye to comprehend that among the graphic descriptions of magical beings and mythical lands are distorted body parts. Bruno Basso explains their engagement with fables, fairytales and fantastic creatures. 'I believe images are waiting to be found in our genetic heritage. We create chaos to make the familiar seem unfamiliar.' He is a proponent of psychoanalyst Carl Jung's theory that there are universal inherited images waiting to be discovered. When these images are allied to those found in myths and fairytales, they become part of a collective unconscious, common to all mankind.

Bruno Basso has no fashion background, but the three years he spent in journalism and as an advertising art director in his native Brazil have instilled a pragmatic approach to the fashion business. 'I'm used to the corporate environment, and I know about business,' he explains. 'Business activates another part of the brain to design, and I understand the mechanics of building a brand, but at the same time I am able to be creative.'

Designs from the 'Succubus and Other Tales' series by Basso & Brooke; 'The King's Fart', and (overleaf) the 'Fable' design and a collection of long scarves. Their work wittily subverts images and narratives from traditional fairytales.

He came to London to study visual anthropology, but two weeks after his arrival he met Christopher Brooke, an English fashion graduate from Kingston who subsequently went on to gain a Masters degree from Central St Martins School of Art. 'Bruno and I have different aesthetics. He has not studied fashion, so he doesn't have the awareness of what has gone before as I do. We are a combination of English eccentric allied to that South American sensitivity to vibrant colour, the spirit of carnival.'

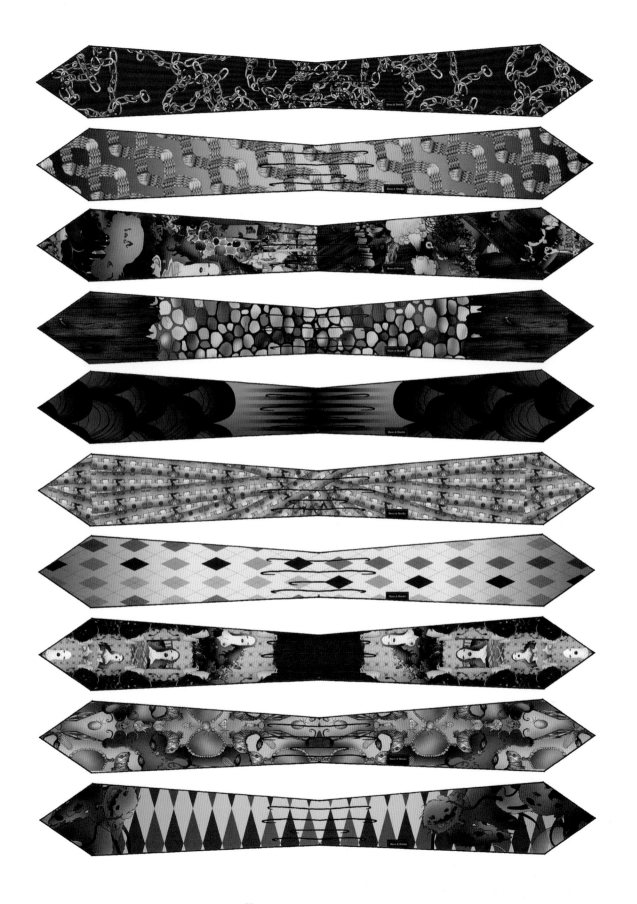

The label Basso & Brooke presented its first catwalk show at London Fashion Week in February 2005. Their almost psychedelic prints, with their juxtaposition of sensuous line and sexual imagery, is redolent of the graphic poster art of 1960s counter-culture, but without the political agenda. That was a period of intense preoccupation with an eclectic mix of influences from Alphonse Mucha and Art Nouveau to Surrealism, fuelled by the effects of hallucinogenic drugs and incorporating imaginary worlds and landscapes. The colour palette is similarly extravagant. Bruno Basso claims to be affected by synaesthesia, a brain condition in which stimuli from one sense are interpreted through another so that, for instance, colours produce sensations associated with sounds. 'I can recognize 2,000 shades of red, 20 shades of white.'

Typical of their style is the dress representing the fairytale heroine Rapunzel emerging from the towering inferno. The dress is printed in a spectrum of colours and embellished with 10 kilograms (22 lb) of Swarovski crystals. Although their prints are about retrieving ancient myths and legends, the processes they use are modern. Christopher Brooke explains: 'We are entering the digital era, where we rely on technology and depend on computers.'

Basso concurs: 'We are 100 per cent digital. We have no romantic ideas about being part of the process of development; anyone could carry out our ideas. We could not have done our stuff five years ago.' All the sampling of garments and prints is done in Italy. Brooke likes to design three-dimensionally on the stand, rather than on paper, and is concerned that the cutting utilizes the print. 'When we started printing we would do an all-over print and cut out the garment, but now all our print designs are engineered to fit the pattern piece.' He is a great admirer of the work done by Celia Birtwell and Ossie Clark in the early 1970s. 'They were the perfect synthesis of print and garment. You need to reference the past to see how you've progressed, to see if you have taken it as far as it will go.' Basso & Brooke's desire to communicate their particular aesthetic is echoed in the ideas expressed in their 'pirate dress'. High up on the bodice is the image of a galleon, sailing on the tempestuous seas of the long, flowing skirts. It represents the challenge without which no fairytale is complete: the quest for affirmation.

'Tempest' from the 'Succubus and other Tales' series by Basso & Brooke.

Rory Crichton's interpretation and sinuous composition of Giles Deacon's illustrations for the ironic, neo-gothic print collection 'Disco Jacobean Fairy Tale'.

The fairytale images of Giles Deacon's first collection under his own name in February 2004, entitled 'Disco Jacobean Fairytale', are leavened by a sense of humour and a knowingness of how far to push the boundaries of the fantastical and the commercial. The former designer for the Gucci Group and Bottega Veneta, Deacon spent his childhood among the dramatic scenery of a remote part of the Lake District in north-west England, a background reflected in the almost gothic interpretations of nature that were a feature of the acclaimed collection. His fantastical prints – of a Beardsley-like quality of line and arcane subject matter, with cobwebs, fairies, twigs and trees – were created in conjunction with long-term collaborator Rory Crichton. 'The first collection was a labour of love,' Crichton recalls. 'The collection was very literal, and we had a bit of a laugh. We share a sense of humour, and we push each other to see how far we can go. We wanted people to sit up at the fashion show. People like to be entertained.'

The prints were executed at the Glasgow School of Art. Crichton is rigorous in his pursuit of high-quality production, which also involves seeking out small-scale craftmakers, and this is reflected in the almost couture-like quality of the clothes. Crichton also makes the drawings for the jacquard weaves, which are then created by the Suffolk weaving firm Stephen Walters & Sons.

Designers have always felt an affinity with telling stories. There is no simpler route to the human imagination than to allow it to explore the myths and mark-making of other cultures, places and times, and fashion is perfectly placed to utilize this. Myth-making occurs in every culture, and whether rooted in history or fantasy, it infiltrates the fashion process. 'Foreign' artefacts too are compelling, but unlike the days of colonialism, when art and artefacts were plundered from distant countries in a desire to return with trophies for Western museums, the designer now places equal value on the trivial. There is no hierarchy of taste; ephemera will be given the same respect as something ancient and fiscally valuable. The designer endeavours to create a narrative that the wearer can then borrow, to wear and remove at will. For the designer, exchanging cultures by valuing and utilizing the specialist skills of the indigenous craftmakers is one way of combating the potentially 'imperialist' overtones of the relationship.

chapter five
graphics
and graffiti

Living in an increasingly urban environment, we are subject to a
multiplicity of chaotic visual references in our daily life, from the
saturation of the city street with advertising billboards and graffiti to
the complex and sophisticated graphics of computer games.
This plethora of images from popular culture inevitably infiltrates all
levels of the design process. Consequently, modern print design
also knows no boundaries. Where once couture houses relied upon
the staff of their ateliers to produce exquisite and labour-intensive
embroidery, designers are now eager to juxtapose traditional
embellishments with those from an eclectic range of sources.

'In no other form of society in history has there been such a concentration of images, such a density of visual messages. One may remember or forget these messages but briefly one takes them in, and for a moment they stimulate the imagination by way of either memory or expectation.'

John Berger (1926-)[i]

Opposite: *the power of a simple motif when replicated is shown in Alexander Henry Fabric's multi-coloured print 'Countdown'.* Previous page: *Rory Crichton for Luella – 'Voodoo Doll'.*

The relative simplicity of the screen-printing process has democratized design. Even more accessible in promulgating singular aesthetics is the Internet. E-commerce facilitates the realization of a delusory individualism through mass customization, enabling the consumer to specify their personal requirements in terms of image, colour or text. Innovations such as heat transfer printing, a method that employs heat and pressure to transfer an image from paper to fabric, is yet another process that enables the individual literally to make his or her mark. Such is the eagerness of designers to utilize and embrace new technology that companies such as Reflective Technology Industries produce their 'retroflective ink' (which throws light back to its source, an effect similar to the 'cat's eyes' used in road safety) in kit form for £15. The accessibility of these processes means that anyone can access the means to showcase their creativity or their viewpoint.

4521045210452104
146581465814658
063140631406314
17985179851798

LOOK AT ME

*The ultimate in personalised
fashion, the 'Be a Bag' range by
designer Anya Hindmarch.*

This modern interaction between customer and designer is evidenced in the
successful marketing of handbags. The customer emails a digital image, or submits
a photograph, to entrepreneurial opportunists who use them to customize bags
with personal photographs – an idea first attributed to British designer Anya
Hindmarch. The 'Be a Bag' personal photo-bag service started in 2001.

The phenomenon of the designer handbag has led to print becoming one of the
media that designers engaged with in the search for novelty. Couture houses such
as Dior and Chanel are impelled to provide the must-have bag of the season, and
its concomitant waiting list. The French luxury-goods brand Louis Vuitton, with
its history of high-quality luggage and leather accessories, plays with the iconic
nature of the product by collaborating with artists and designers who incorporate
the logo into their own aesthetic. Founded in 1854 by Louis Vuitton, by the end
of the 19th century the company was already troubled by imitators. Georges
Vuitton, the founder's son, designed and patented the world-renowned logo,
making L V luggage among the first manufactured products to bear the name of
the brand on the outside. A century after the registration of the Louis Vuitton
trademark, the company has engaged with radical artists and designers such as
Tracy Emin, Julie Verhoeven and Takashi Murakami to recreate and celebrate the
instantly identifiable L V logo. Murakami's combination of high art and low
culture has a contemporary force that infiltrates all aspects of Western design.
Obsessed with Japanese Anime and Manga comics, and embracing the influence
of 1960s pop artists such as Andy Warhol, Murakami's work is underpinned by his
training in Nihon-ga, a 19th-century Japanese painting technique. He now works
for the Kaikai Kiki Corporation, producing kitsch and neon bright images, and
artefacts from watches to sculptures. His idiosyncratic cartoon-like figures in acid-
bright colours, juxtaposed with the L V logo, can be seen in the range of 'eye love'
bags he designed in collaboration with Louis Vuitton. Launched in 2003, the bags
now produce a turnover of $300 million.

Integrating text into the body of a garment is a potent means of expression; the
garment has to be 'read' twice, once as an item of clothing and once as a
narrative. The T-shirt is a blank canvas. As a fashion classic in plain white it is a
wardrobe staple for both sexes. Embellished with images or text it is used for
promulgating ideas, promoting brands and music tours, or used as a message

board for subversion or misplaced wit. Originally worn as part of the uniform of the US Navy in 1899, the T-shirt was appropriated by Marlon Brando and James Dean in the 1950s, propelling it to the status of non-conformist and anti-establishment. It was tie-dyed and dip-dyed in the psychedelic 1960s, printed with slogans by Tommy Roberts in 1968, and ripped and shredded and screen-printed with the face of Johnny Rotten by Sex Pistols graphic designer Jamie Reid during the punk years. When designer Katherine Hamnett, on being introduced to the then Prime Minister Margaret Thatcher at a Downing Street dinner party, wore a supersize T-shirt declaring that '58% DON'T WANT PERSHING' (referring to the US nuclear missiles then based in Britain), it was a moment captured by the world's press.

Text can be playful, rude, informative, witty, instructive, threatening, or even confessional, but it demands to be read. At its most perfunctory it commands attention on the simplest T-shirt, or it can provide a perfect vehicle for heartfelt polemic, as in John Galliano's design for Christian Dior in 2005 with the simple message, 'Dior not War'. At its most sophisticated, it is the specially written newspaper printed on cloth for Galliano by fellow ex-Central St Martins School of Art graduates Stephanie Nash and Anthony Michael, containing in-jokes, a recurring component of his designs.

Concern with the social and political implications of the fashion establishment causes a number of designers to opt out of mass-produced fashion, subverting its processes by appropriating logos and brands. They replace spectacular and costly catwalk shows and styled glossy magazine shoots with DVD magazines and alternative venues to show their clothes.

British designer Russell Sage's critical exposition of the fashion business was manifest in his patterned dresses constructed from real banknotes. 'I can't bear the lies about fashion. Anything anyone knows about fashion comes through the media.' His dislike of fashion hype is clear; the season after his graduation from the fashion Masters programme at Central St Martins School of Art, he held a party in Brick Lane, styled by Katie Grand. 'I couldn't afford lighting, the clothes were badly made, but we all had raw enthusiasm. I attached logos with elephant tape to clothes, which predated the Vuitton graffiti bags, ripped up the linings of Burberry clothes (who actually tried to sue me), and then they did the same things themselves six months later!'

A playful appropriation of the power of newsprint: blue-jean corset, grey cotton catsuit and oversize newspaper print trousers and cardigan, all by John Galliano.

135

A statement against mass-produced fashion, art brand 'Noki' subverts logos and customises second-hand clothes to make one-off artworks.

Noki, the 'art brand', is also concerned with the consumerist, throwaway nature of fashion, evident in his cut-and-paste garment designs that reappropriate fashion-brand logos. The designer, when working as a stylist at MTV in the late 1990s, had something of an epiphany. 'I had a realization of the power of the subliminal message I was pushing. I was infiltrating the viewers' minds with brand recognition. I had become part of the problem.'

The designer created the persona of 'Noki' ('ikon' spelled backwards) in an attempt to rehabilitate himself. 'I decided that the best way to celebrate brands was to play the reappropriation game, subverting the message and challenging the norm. I take second-hand branded T-shirts and customize or redesign them into one-off pieces that challenge the original intent of a new homogenized multiple-branded product. It is the things that have happened to the T-shirt that render it important, not the logo on the front of the original factory-made pattern piece from a colour dye batch. After the processes of wear and tear, washing and sunbleaching, shrinkage and seam twisting, stains and holes, the instinct is to throw it away. But rejection breeds invention. When I look at a second-hand T-shirt, if there is a stain, it guides me to stick a stencil or screen print there, thus reclaiming all the things we are not supposed to like.'

'GRAFFITI IS AN ACTIVITY, NOT A STYLE'[ii]

Ironically, the activities of subversive designers are swiftly incorporated into the mainstream, and an anti-corporate ethos is counterbalanced by the ability, and even the desire, of brand labels to co-opt and absorb the ideas of its detractors. Commodification of street style was confirmed with Marc Jacobs's decision to invite the American avant-garde fashion designer Stephen Sprouse to design graffiti bags for luxury brand Louis Vuitton in 2000. This signified a revival of interest in the tags and stencils of the street, and rendered something precious and covetable out of what is socially, if not artistically, considered undesirable.

During the 1960s and early 1970s graffiti in Western urban environments was rarely concerned with aesthetics. Scrawled in inaccessible places, on bridges or alongside railway lines, graffiti gave voice to disaffected youth or the political activist. In the United States it was used to define the territory of street gangs in the larger cities. From 1968, when the first 'tag' appeared, graffiti began also to become an art form. Its legitimization came in the mid-1970s when New York's subway trains drew the attention of the contemporary art world, and the taggers were courted by gallery owners and museum curators. By 1980 Jean-Michel Basquiat, under the tag name SAMO© ('Same Old Shit'), began selling canvases and no longer worked the streets. Keith Haring, who had studied at the New York School of Visual Arts, exchanged the unused black paper advertising panels of the subway for canvas, T-shirts, posters and murals, elevating the visual vernacular and influencing mainstream fashion. Brand managers, always eager to embrace cultural opposition, are incorporating graffiti into clothes, a move fuelled by its relationship to hip-hop culture. Adidas, Puma, Stussy and Carhartt all borrow from graffiti's aesthetic, and the graffiti print denim jackets designed by Wale Adeyemi inspired a flood of high-street copies when they were seen being worn by the footballer David Beckham and his son Brooklyn. British fashion designer Luella Bartley's autumn/winter look for 2004 included prints of aerosol-spray graffiti swirls.

'THE STRIPE DOESN'T WAIT, DOESN'T STAND STILL' [iii]

Work in progress: a 'mood board' montage, indicating the possible mix of images, colours and patterns for a range by fashion label Paul Smith.

While graffiti is still an illegal activity, stripes now convey nothing more threatening than patterned cloth, though this was not always the case, since they were once traditionally perceived as transgressive. The medieval stripe represented disorder, and was relegated to 'outcasts or reprobates'.[iv] Even today comic-strip burglars, naughty boys and convicts are customarily represented as wearing horizontally striped clothes. Apart from this appropriation by the outsider, stripes are used as a warning device for such things as pedestrian crossings, and to define exclusion zones.

Stripes are the simplest of all patterns, a series of parallel lines going in one direction, a rhythmic surface that indicates movement. Stripes are always given visual priority. This not only makes them useful environmentally, but it also results in the wearer of striped clothes either standing out from the crowd, or being easily identified as part of a group (the businessman's aggressively striped shirt, the schoolchild's blazer). Stripes are generally artificial, and rarely occur in nature. They are a manmade construct, evidence of a desire to make a culturally significant mark. Visually we are programmed to seek out straight lines, and this innate preference for order makes stripes one of the most satisfying and versatile print motifs, where variation is reliant on proportion and colour. The signature coloured stripes of British designer Paul Smith are instantly identifiable – whether on bags, furniture or ceramics – to the extent that when multi-coloured stripes are seen in any other context they bring to mind the 'Paul Smith' label.

Paul Smith is renowned for classic garments that also demonstrate a discreet eccentricity that is essentially British. In 1970 he opened his first shop in his hometown of Nottingham, and in 1976 he showed his menswear collection for the first time in Paris. The opening of the first Paul Smith store in London's Covent Garden in 1979 coincided with the election of Mrs Thatcher, a resurgence in the money markets of the City, and subsequent changes in social attitudes. Although his suits for men became standard wear for the 1980s young urban professional – the 'yuppie' – his aesthetic has always included a witty and subversive eye for detail together with an idiosyncratic and entirely personal use of colour and texture. As the Paul Smith style infiltrated mainstream retail chains, his company developed a

The final design, combining the signature Paul Smith stripes with a border of photorealistic garden flowers.

greater emphasis on fashion, and in 1993 he introduced a womenswear collection that gave full rein to his desire to incorporate sophisticated prints that have a vintage resonance. With the opening of the Westbourne Grove shop in London's Notting Hill area in 1998, the designer introduced another retail concept, that of the shop as home, and since then he has continued to diversify into home furnishings. His design for the Rug Company of multi-coloured swirling stripes has become a design classic. Stripes are integral to his spring/summer 2005 collection; together with a multiplicity of florals, the designs exemplify the process by which disparate design sources can be brought together.

Sandra Hill, head of womenswear design at the company, emphasizes that print is the first priority when designing a new collection, and that designing with print makes particular demands.

'Print and colour are the first consideration, always. Designing for men, the print is enough, and it is preferable to keep to a straightforward jacket and trousers. Print design for women is much more complex, and the print has to work with the garment.'

She describes the process. 'At the beginning of the season Paul invites all the designers to discuss and brainstorm ideas for the season's theme. There may be more than one. Ideas will have been collected from images and books; a dress picked up at a flea market, a painting, or even a pair of old socks can spark inspiration for the next season's colours. Once the theme has been identified, the designers research the whole subject using the Internet, books, antiques, fabric archives. There is a travel budget, so the designers get to go to other countries for inspiration. Museums, flea markets, galleries or even the local charity shops are visited. The research or inspiration can come from almost anywhere in the form of photographs, fabric, antiques, wallpaper etc.'

Once all this research has been collected, the designer creates a 'mood board', which consists of images, possible designs and a colour palette, and the final design is chosen.

The chosen design could be a drawing, a photograph or an object, and it is then either scanned or a transparency is produced. The print designer will develop the artwork, usually on a Macintosh computer using PhotoShop or Illustrator. They

may do several colourways to choose from, or several variations. The design has to take into account the end garment. If it is for shirting fabric, any repeat in the print must correspond with the width of the fabric. A scarf design requires borders, and if it is a placement print, the designer has to work to a garment pattern. Scale, repeat and colour are all taken into account.

The printing technique depends on the type of design and on the number of colour separations there are. More than eight can become expensive when screen-printing. A simple graphic design will usually involve traditional printing methods, and rotary screens are engraved. These methods can include pigment prints, discharge printing, or using reactive dyes – depending on the design and the quality of the fabric (whether it is synthetic or natural).

Once the printing technique is determined, the price, print minimum and delivery date of the fabric are taken into account. 'We use a diversity of printers,' says Hill, 'each have their own specialisms. According to the technique required, the printer is selected and we send out the artwork. They develop a computer-aided printout in full repeat. This needs to be approved by the designer for scale, repeat, clarity and colour, although the exact colour may be different on the fabric. Once this trial is approved the printer either engraves the design onto screens or cylinders, or in the case of photographic prints they will go straight to digital output.'

Strike-offs are small sample trials done to test the design on cloth and to match the colours required. 'Once the strike-off is approved for colour and technique, a minimum sample length of 30–50 metres is ordered. This is checked against the original strike-off, as occasionally a bigger run will produce differences from a small trial. This printed fabric length is then made into the required garment samples that are shown in the show rooms and the catwalk shows.' Before the full production run for retail distribution, further checks are carried out to maintain colour and quality of the fabric. 'These can vary from slight changes in colour to a discussion about the finish of the fabric. Once these amendments are agreed between the designer and the printer, production of the new range can go ahead. It is constantly tested and quality-controlled. The fabric is then sent to the garment manufacturers to be made up, and shipped to one of our many shops.'

Polychromatic warp-knitted stripes were for many years the unmistakable signature of the Italian company Missoni. This demonstrated Rosita and Tai

Starting with two knitting machines in the 1950s, the Missoni company originally specialised in distinctive stripe knit dresses. Now a global fashion dynasty, their aesthetic embraces all aspects of pattern.

A graphic interpretation of an everyday object: 'Shoe Review' by Alexander Henry Fabrics.

Missoni's virtuosity with the knitting machine. A family company sited in the hills above Milan, Missoni was founded by the couple in 1953 and was one of the first labels to distance knitwear from its frumpy, artisanal image and place it at the forefront of 1970s' fashionable glamour. The company's multicoloured stripes and zigzags in effervescent space-dyed yarns were very much part of the desire of that era to return to European smartness in the wake of the tattered remnants of hippie culture. The label, alongside others such as Pucci, languished to some extent in the 1980s and 1990s, when fashion preferred the minimalist aesthetic of Helmut Lang and Prada. Since a radical refocusing by their daughter Angela in 1998, when she took over as creative director, the label has moved into the 21st century by extending its range beyond knitwear and incorporating print into its body-revealing garments.

A combination of acutely observed drawings and Russian folklore motifs in this illustration by Sarah Hodgson, which references aspects of contemporary life and modern-day sins, such as 'Sloth'.

PICTURE THIS

In contrast to the sophisticated imagery of computer-aided graphics and dextrous digital imagery is the work of the illustrator. The appeal of this lo-fi aesthetic is a response to the singular nature of the illustrator's vision, and the immediacy of the mark. Hand-drawn illustrations utilize the fast-disappearing art of drawing, and have all the sensitivity of the idiosyncratic and the personal. They are a feature of the work of Sarah Hodgson, a graduate of the Royal College of Art. Her work documents popular culture, mediated through a 1960s sensibility of Pop and Op art; the record sleeve of the Beatles' album *Sgt. Pepper's Lonely Hearts Club Band*, designed by London artist Peter Blake in 1967, is one of her inspirations. The graphic style and the use of flat, opaque colour characteristic of 1960s' modernism can be seen in her sequence of illustrations of the seven deadly

147

*London iconography and
contemporary politicians feature in
Sarah Hodgson's 'Wrath' print.*

sins featuring such 21st-century obsessions as celebrity culture and body image. Her work embraces such diverse images as the Royal Family and Krispy Kreme doughnuts.

'I'm really intrigued by political cartoons, and find that drawing very simply, with a ball-point pen or felt tip, is a really free way of exploring ideas through documenting detail – often in a very subversive way. I'm also influenced by music posters from the 1960s, which I source on the Portobello market.'

Collaging together thirty or forty drawings, the designer then scans them and manipulates them in PhotoShop, trying out various colourways.

'It would take twenty screens and five weeks to produce a design without the computer. I have really moved away from the layering and textures of my painterly background to embrace a graphic quality in my work.'

Hodgson's series of images featuring London transport and tourist destinations has all the quirkiness of a cartoon but, when juxtaposed with traditional textile motifs such as a border of roses, it extends beyond social comment.

London-based artists and designers Julie Verhoeven and Natasha Law are at the forefront of those responsible for a reappraisal of the art of fashion illustration, usurped in the recent past by the authority of the photographic image. Bobby Hillson, founding course director of the Master's programme in fashion at Central St Martins School of Art, is also a practising fashion illustrator, and remembers how it fell out of favour in the 1960s. 'At the end of the 1960s photography replaced the work of the fashion illustrator. Generally people wouldn't buy from a drawing, and illustration wasn't used at all in magazines.'[iv]

The fluctuation of the popularity of illustration within the fashion press means that illustrators have to extend the boundaries of their practice to sustain a long career. As designer and illustrator Julie Verhoeven confirms, 'Although there has been something of a resurgence in fashion illustration over the past few years, there isn't enough work around to do only that.'

Rather than illustration being merely a vehicle for showing clothes, the illustrator now has to engage with all aspects of the design, imparting an element of narrative, sensuality or whimsy to create a very personal response to

the clothes. This broadening of the context of the work results in illustrative skills being used on the garments themselves. Julie Verhoeven was invited by the Italian manufacturer Gibo in 2000 to design a range of clothing featuring her idiosyncratic and delicately psychedelic images, all rooted in her commitment to drawing. 'My passion is drawing; it is the starting point for everything.' She is not, however, a casual sketcher. 'The setting has to be right for me to work. I put myself at a remove. I like to really concentrate by cutting off the rest of the world, and have to have solitude. I work in the studio to very loud music to block out distractions, and not much light. I'm not a big fan of daylight.' Conversely there is a vibrant, generous and happy quality about Verhoeven's work that has ensured successful commissions for album covers, fashion advertising and animations for pop videos as well as illustration for magazines and newspapers including *Dazed & Confused*, the *Sunday Times* and the *Face*. She has also worked as a designer for Ghost, Philip Treacy and Richard Tyler, and was recently a consultant for Cacharel.

Initially enrolling at Medway College (now the Kent Institute) visiting tutor Howard Tangye suggested that she join his fashion illustration classes at Central St Martins School of Art. At the same time she was working as an assistant to John Galliano. 'I hadn't got a clue how a designer worked, and didn't realize that John was exceptional in the amount of research he does for a collection. At the beginning of each collection he would spend a couple of weeks in the library at the London College of Fashion or the V&A and I'd go with him to carry the books and do some photocopying. It was a great grounding. I did a bit of everything: print designs, T-shirts, artwork for invitations to the shows.'

Verhoeven follows the same process. 'I loved the research, and that is why my work is so heavily research-based. I love excess, I'll find a million pictures, a lot of which might be unnecessary, but then influences come to the surface.'

Artist and designer Julie Verhoeven is at the forefront of the early 21st-century reappraisal of the skills of the illustrator. Her calligraphic, multi-layered images evidence a waywardness in choice of subject. Overleaf: the artfully seductive 'Pandora' and 'Phantom', both executed for Italian fashion label Gibo.

Verhoeven's drawing materials are traditional. 'I always feel comfortable with a Pilot pen, pencil or charcoal, but I jump between different things. I enjoy collage, I like things to be multi-layered. I never use the computer, it's too slow, too frustrating, you lose momentum and I like to build up speed. I make it difficult for myself. People have such a romantic idea about the artist and designer in the studio. I love it, but it's hard work to reproduce something as it looks, and still inject something of oneself. I know in my head how I want it to look, and

Left: 'Sun', a Natasha Law design
for fashion label Frostfrench.
Below: 'Rick Shah' by Natasha
Law, courtesy of Space.

sometimes it comes out differently. Designing for Gibo is no different from my illustration work in that I treat the designs as pictures that should stand alone as a drawing. I lose interest if I have to start putting things in repeat. I like to print on chiffon or georgette, because that reflects the multi-layering of my artwork. It's all about movement, intensity, and the play on colour.'

Natasha Law is renowned for her print designs for the fashion label Frostfrench, but her practice also includes painting, photography, graphics and illustration. Her paintings are bold, containing beautifully observed figures of women cropped tightly into the frame, sensual, assertive, and with a singular message, such as 'pink heels' or 'slip strap.' 'There is an interaction between painting and illustrating. Painting is a way of looking between the lines.'

Law enrolled at Camberwell College of Art to study graphics. 'I never liked using the computer. I used the photocopier as a design tool, transposing lines onto photographs, changing scale, diffusing the image. When I upgraded my computer recently, I lost a lot of my work, and I went back to literally cutting and pasting, playing with marker pens, using the photocopier again. Great things can happen when you start improvising.'

She also relishes the immediacy of screen printing. 'I love the whole process. It can be such an ad hoc thing to do – it's so simple, you can do it on the kitchen table. It's almost like the simplicity of leaving a pair of scissors lying in the sunlight on photographic paper: the image just appears.'

Broad-based as her practice is, Law's commissions are generally concerned with depicting the female figure – young, seductive and glamorous. 'I don't depict real life. You become well known for a particular style, and it can be quite hard to break away from that. I can draw bicycles, too.'

Graphic print design is all about communication, and as such it has an ongoing role in the designer's relationship with the world. Whether she or he is articulating contemporary concerns or proselytizing in straightforward text, making their mark with graffiti, or preoccupied with describing a complex image in a creative manner, it is less to do with texture and manipulation of cloth and all to do with surfaces. It is, above all, flat. There is a simplicity and logic to graphics that observes constraints and does away with extraneous detail. It is intrinsically urban: straight lines are, after all, a man-made construct, and therefore the opposite of natural.

chapter six
vintage

Vintage dressing can have many meanings. There is the appropriation of garments from the past worn with a modern sensibility, as described by American designer Marc Jacobs: 'Today, it's not about retro. You can be dressed in Sixties, Seventies, Forties, Fifties, Thirties, and not look like you're trying to recreate the past if you have that kind of sensibility.'[1] 'Vintage' can mean classic couture from Cameron Silver's influential store Decades in California, or equally a 1960s Pucci shirt from Steven Philip's west London vintage boutique Rellik. What they share is that they are clothes from the past worn with a contemporary bravura, and divorced from any idea of 'retro' or romanticism.

'Creativity is a process of interpreting our history and the world around us. Designers are not the ultimate creators; we are the result of what has gone before.'

Allegra Hicks (2005)

Previous page: design by *Alexander Henry Fabrics.* Right: *two designs by Christopher Bailey for Burberry Prorsum, referencing the English propensity for traditional vintage floral prints and a relaxed silhouette.*

Vintage fashion, however, can also describe a romantic connection to fashion history, with designers borrowing ideas from the past as a source of inspiration for contemporary collections, which may consequently evoke a certain mood of time and place, or quality of craftsmanship. It is a sensibility that instinctively values the old above the new. When 'romanticism' finds expression in the resurrection of vintage clothing items it can become mannerist, even extending to an engagement with the cultural values and sense of atmosphere of former periods. Perhaps vintage clothing is meaningless without these invisible connections – or at least, new layers of meaning are revealed by them. Interpretation depends upon the designer. The regular reappearance of the 1920s–1930s bias-cut tea dress in soft-focus florals may have connotations of the delights of the boudoir, or it could be an element of Marc Jacobs's 1993 definitive and ground-breaking Grunge collection. Conversely, it may imply wholesome pre-war leisurely afternoons taking tea in the garden. It has inspired designers as diverse as John Galliano and Christopher Bailey – the latter creative director of Burberry since 2001. 'At Burberry we take the craft of making both fabric and clothes very seriously, and our culture of textiles here in England is second to none, and can be nothing but inspiring.' Burberry offers a uniquely British style and quality that exports successfully to both Japan and Italy where wearing a traditional British label has tremendous cachet. Burberry's sales in Asia account for more than 26 per cent of its turnover, and the US share amounts to 23 per cent.[ii] 'At Burberry we do combine those worlds of strong history and a rich heritage with a very modern sense of dressing, a mix of very classic, traditional things, and putting your own sexy, street or chi-chi stamp on it.'[iii] Here, 'vintage' has the classic definition of something from the past of high quality that is the best of its type.

PARADIGMS LOST

In periods of rapid change and uncertain futures there is consolation
to be found in recognizing the familiar. Nostalgia is rooted in
sentiment, and this wistful affection for the past animates the yearning
for its trappings; houses, interiors, and clothes might all be recognized
as evoking a particular era. The Greek poet Hesiod wrote in the 8th
century BC of a 'age of gold' – the halcyon days of an eternal
springtime – which he contrasted with the degenerate 'age of iron' in
which he lived. He recognized humankind's innate desire to return to
a place of imagined serenity and safety. When referring to clothing,
vintage does not mean second-hand or recycled. It is about embracing
the known; unostentatious, faded, and quaint. In this context it is an
idiosyncratic way of dressing that is not hard-edged or controlled, but
homespun, faded and eclectic.

This mode of dressing is related to the oppositional dress of the
bohemian, a word with its roots in the Romantic period of the early
19th century, a movement representing a profound unease with
bourgeois values and in love with the idea of the wayward genius.
Bohemian dress was seen as a sign of artistic sensitivity, an
acknowledgement that creativity was divorced from preoccupations
with grooming or observing social niceties. In Britain and North
America bohemianism found expression in the romantic rural vision of
the Arts and Crafts movement at the end of the 19th century, when
many writers, philosophers and artists launched a simple back-to-
nature ethos that presaged the hippies of the 1960s. A multiplicity of
print is integral to this artisan-inspired look, a cohesive coming
together of pattern and colour that is the very opposite of co-
ordinated and sober groomed perfection. The creative outsider,
expressing disaffection through eccentricity of dress, is reacting to the
accessible, the mass-produced and the modern. Clothes are found, or
inherited, or handcrafted, or discovered in attics or thrift shops, or
even at car-boot and garage sales. More likely they are now purchased
from internet trading sites such as e-Bay.

Notions of vintage have a resonance in the eclectic use of colour and pattern in the contemporary collections of Dries van Noten and Marni. Designer Ann-Louise Roswald defines its perennial appeal. 'Fashion pundits are always saying that the Boho look will die, but it is always around in some form or another, because women like it.'

However, vintage design is not only associated with faded florals and the 'gently used' fragments of past glories. It can also be associated with the activity of 'thrifting'. Bay Garnett – stylist for Matthew Williamson – is, with Kira Jolliffe, co-editor of *Cheap Date*, a London and New York magazine devoted to the activity that she describes as a way of developing a personal style. Wearing clothes sourced by thrifting can be a self-styled, idiosyncratic way of staying ahead of the game 'in a way that fashion can't provide'. In an age of increasingly available and excessively priced fashion 'must haves', promulgated through a celebrity-obsessed media, dressing in this way is an assertion of a personal style that may not involve extreme expenditure, but certainly requires a gifted and confident eye. It is a style that is inherently personal, involving the collection of garments that lend a narrative to the wearer. Authenticity makes these items precious, so provenance is all important. What distinguishes these clothes from those found in retail outlets and vintage stores is their exclusivity; they are not available to all. 'Thrifting means sourcing something for yourself, whereas vintage is culled from second-hand and is more expensive and less exciting. You have to be obsessive about it: when I lived in New York I devoted every day in my lunch break when I worked in an office, and every weekend. Thrifting gives you an independent take on fashion; it is the best fashion training for developing an "eye".' Garnett has set in motion many trends, from woven belts worn low on the hips to discovering unusual prints. 'One of my favourite items I've found is a banana-printed top that I got from Cancer Care in New York. I wore it for two years before using it in a shoot for British *Vogue* in May 2003 when I styled Kate Moss.' Once something has become mainstream, she loses interest. 'Designers copy prints because it's safe, they know how it's going to turn out. When fashion cottons on it can become boring. I don't want to be fashionable, it's not what I do. To me, clothes are a canvas of self-expression.' However, thrifting and designer clothes are not mutually exclusive. 'They have to be clothes I like, not just because they're fashionable. I'm very specific in my taste. I don't go on any waiting list.'

Bay Garnett in one of her favourite thrift finds. The banana-printed top was first seen in a fashion story she styled for British Vogue *in 2003, photographed by Juergen Teller. Modelled by Kate Moss, the print, shorts and low-slung leather belt have subsequently been enormously influential.*

'A BOUTIQUE EXPERIENCE, NOT A JUMBLE SALE' *Steven Philip*

Steven Phillip originally had a stall on London's Portobello Market until the burgeoning vintage movement led him to open Rellik with two friends. His shop specialises in pieces that represent significant fashion moments.

Specialist shops have opened for those who want the look but don't have the time or the 'eye' to seek out what makes something second-hand special. According to Steven Philip, owner of west London store Rellik, the desire for vintage fashion arose as a response to the brand-crazy days of the 1980s and 1990s. 'In 1989 there was a bland and grey minimalism. Everyone was after the same thing, and people were living on credit. Limited-edition bags were everywhere, even though there was supposed to be a waiting list. At a party there would be the same bags, the same Chanel dress. There are always a few people who want to stand out from the crowd and say, "I'm not going to buy into this".'

These evocations of the past find their way into mainstream fashion as contemporary designers rework vintage fashion into their own collections. 'Designers buying and copying vintage is one of the biggest unspoken secrets. The thing about clothes from the 1940s to the 1970s is that there was a great deal of experimentation going on, and also a great attention to detail. There is an encyclopedia of print in vintage.'

Philip believes that we live in a culture that is increasingly homogenized, where originality is quickly seized upon and copied. 'There is good magpie and bad magpie. To be truly inspired by something is different to taking a little bit of everything from everywhere. There is no creativity in that "pick & mix" attitude.' Certainly the roll call of revamped styles from the last century alone provides evidence of the designer's propensity to replicate the past; Art Nouveau, Art Deco, modernism, Pop art, punk, and the cult of the logo are all continuing sources of inspiration for the print designer.

There are also the enduring fashion legends – such as Audrey Hepburn, Grace Kelly and Marlene Dietrich – who continue to be represented everywhere in popular culture. Philip describes his customers as increasingly design literate. 'The customers who buy from me may not know their fashion history, but they are very fashion aware. They might see a photograph of Jackie Kennedy on a yacht wearing Pucci in the 1960s, and think she looks chic and glamorous, and they want that look, without really knowing anything about Pucci.'

A row of precious garments from the legendary Italian print label Emilio Pucci hang on the rails inside the vintage store Rellik.

The upsurge in demand during the 1990s for legendary vintage label Pucci, one of the most identifiable print designers of the 20th century, regenerated interest in the company, and in 2000 the French luxury conglomerate L V M H (Louis Vuitton-Moët Hennessy) bought a majority stake. In the late 1940s and the 1950s, when haute couture implied a ladylike, constructed elegance and artifice, the Marquis Emilio Pucci di Barsento began designing relaxed, glamorous leisurewear in innovative lightweight fabrics and brilliant prints. Trained as a pilot in the Italian air force, Pucci had no background in design when, in 1947, he was photographed skiing in St Moritz dressed in a ski suit he had designed himself.

By the 1960s his clothes had became synonymous with the new jet age, an enduring status symbol worn by style setters and celebrated beauties such as Marilyn Monroe (she wanted to be buried in her favourite Pucci), Audrey Hepburn and Jackie Kennedy Onassis. He introduced stretch into fabrics; 'Emilioform' was an elasticized silk shantung that he developed in 1960, which liberated women from constricting girdles and layers of underwear to reveal a new athleticism.

His designs captured the new post-war desire for travel. Weighing less than 250 grams (8 oz), the clothes were portable, required no ironing, and the dazzling prints reflected the exotic, colour-filled horizons of his jet-setting clientele.

He drew his inspiration from many sources; Renaissance paintings, the regalia of the Palio race in Siena, or the colours and patterns indigenous to an exotic country. These images were always filtered through the medium of his signature style – abstract, non-figurative form and psychedelic swirls of colour, often controlled by borders of contrasting print and signed 'Emilio'.

In 1963 Noel Barber wrote in *Cosmopolitan* that 'Pucci has special colour shorthand and can create intricate colour patterns for as many as a hundred scarves an hour. He draws the sketches for four or five scarves, they are photographed, and twenty prints of each black and white are enlarged to the size of a scarf. The hundred photo prints are scattered on the office floor. He has lots of bottles of coloured ink, each one is numbered, and he says he knows the colours by heart. With a girl following him, Pucci walks among the prints, pointing out certain spaces on the design, calling out

numbers. The assistant marks the correct number in the space and each print is then coloured … They paint the design by filling in the spaces according to the number, then the designs go to the printers near Como.'[iv]

The desire for Pucci's status clothes was undermined by the plethora of cheap copies on the market, and fashion moved on to embrace a new eclecticism with the burgeoning hippie movement. Travel became a matter of hitching to India, not jet-setting to Europe. However, Pucci remained enormously influential and inspired both Stephen Sprouse and Gianni Versace. In 2002, ten years after the marquis's death, Christian Lacroix was appointed artistic director of the firm, and he helped bring about an upturn in sales. Laudomia Pucci, Emilio's daughter, is now the director of the fashion empire and continues to be preoccupied by colour. 'Having grown up surrounded by colour, I'd say it was a language for me, a manner of expression. What are my favourites? I'm often inspired by the colours of St Petersburg's Palaces – blues, greens, pinks, oranges – but also my father's favourite colours, which include all shades of aqua, fuchsia, lilac, lime and the sunny colours of our Mediterranean sea and sun. I'm not sure why he became such a colourist; perhaps it was his Russian blood (inherited from his own father). Think Fabergé! Mix that with his Florentine roots and you get something explosive and irresistible, yet also elegant and romantic.'[v]

The distinctive print designs and simple shapes of Emilio Pucci epitomised leisurewear to a generation of 1960s 'jetsetters'.

Feel like a
woman,
Wear a dress!

Diane Von Furstenberg

A SIGN OF THE TIMES

As with Pucci, the rarity of certain vintage items can lend it a cult status, and propel the designer into relaunching the look. The iconic Diane Von Furstenberg wrap dress first appeared in 1973 in a wood-grain print. It was a time when women were enjoying new-found independence and needed low-maintenance fashion that was suitable for their emergence into the workplace. In an era when women, if not disbarred, were not actively encouraged to wear trousers at work, the simple but sexy wrap dress was the perfect solution. 'Feel like a woman, wear a dress!' became a registered trademark. The dress typified the era of women's sexual and political liberation, and by 1976 some five million had been sold. Cut to flatter, the dress wrapped in front and tied at the waist and was made from drip-dry cotton jersey in instantly recognizable twig and splatter prints. It was effortlessly glamorous, in contrast to the fashion then currently on offer. The designer recalls: 'I had no focus groups, no marketing surveys, no plan. All I had was an instinct that women wanted a fashion option beside hippie clothes, bell bottoms and stiff pant suits that hid their femininity.'[vi]

A design as consistently simple as the wrap dress demands a strong emphasis on the print. 'I love prints. I look for new ideas everywhere, in a man's tie, an old oriental rug, an Art Deco vase, and then adapt the design idea for my fabrics. You can change your entire mood with a different print even though the shape or the silhouette of the dress is the same. For example, you have to feel different in a leopard print than you do in a garden print. I did my first snakeskin in black and brown because those colours seemed natural and they were big sellers. So I decided to do them again, but in bright green and orange and women liked them too, and felt sexy in them. I think the shape of the dress was changed slightly, but the mood of the snakeskin was the same.'[vii]

Despite building up a fashion empire, Diane Von Furstenberg sold her original dress company in 1978 and lost control of her label to licensees in the 1980s. By 1997, when the dress was attracting a new generation of women keen to access the then newly fashionable look of the 1970s, they bought up all the vintage stock. Diane Von Furstenberg relaunched the business and put the dress back into production, this time in silk jersey and with a contemporary range of colours and prints. Investigating her company's archives, in 2004 she reintroduced the twig print from the dress she wore on the cover of *Newsweek* magazine in March 1976.

Diane Von Furstenberg's first advertisment appeared in America's fashion bible Women's Wear Daily *in 1972. It was the beginning of the label's influential edict of no-fuss dressing: 'chic, practical, and seductive'. The signature became a brand.*

Print designer Celia Birtwell influences and inspires contemporary fashion and textile designers. Christopher Bailey commissioned these drawings for the 8th edition of Another Magazine. Overleaf: *two scarf designs from Birtwell's 2005 collection.*

Her fashion collections are no longer limited to 'the dress', but print is still an integral part of her design aesthetic. 'Print is like colour, it enriches the fabric. The cut is what gives fabric movement … it gives life to the fabric.'

The successful relaunching or reappraisal of vintage labels requires timing. Prints define an era: they are just as much of the moment as music, literature or art. The designs of Emilio Pucci and Diane Von Furstenberg were a radical response to the needs of the time. Pucci provided a modern solution to the desire of the newly mobile 'beautiful people', who required leisure clothes that confirmed their athleticism and desire for strong, bright colours after the austerity of the immediate post-war period. Diane Von Furstenberg responded to the requirements of women emerging into the workplace needing sexy but severe good taste to see them through the day. The times are different now, but the modernity of their aesthetic still attracts.

Celia Birtwell and Ossie Clark offered a triumphant synthesis of cut and pattern during the 1960s and 1970s, and their garments are now much sought after by collectors and are housed in museums and costume archives. The turn of the 21st century saw Celia Birtwell's print designs for fashion replicated almost exactly by big-name brands and luxury labels, and she has decided to reclaim her fashion customers after two decades spent devoting her skills to designing prints for interiors. The result is to bring her work to a new audience, attracting the respect of contemporary designers, eager to acknowledge her influence. She is considered by Christopher Bailey to be an icon in the world of print and textiles. Introduced to French fashion house Cacharel by designers Suzanne Clements and Inácio Ribeiro, she found the experience very different from that of working with her then husband, 1960s master of cutting, Ossie Clark. 'I was constantly amazed and surprised by how Ossie interpreted my designs. I still work the same way, drawing the designs onto the figure, often using three or more prints of different scale.'

Historical references have always been important to Birtwell, from the work of Léon Bakst for the Ballets Russes, to the painter Matisse, renowned for his love of textiles. Brought up in a north-eastern corner of France at the heart of the textile industry, Matisse was utterly seduced by the possibilities of clashing patterns and bold colour. He spent his life adding to his collection of textiles, his 'working library'. He painted his models reclining among a plethora of Spanish shawls, tapestries, costumes, Persian carpets, brocades from Algeria, wall hangings,

cushions, and silks, all used as source material for his paintings. His influence has permeated the work of designers from Yves Saint Laurent to Christian Lacroix, including Celia Birtwell. She continues to find him a great source of inspiration. 'When in doubt, look at Matisse. There is serious academic drawing, masked in this portrayal of simplicity.' Her contemporary designs show the same ebullience and joy in colour. 'Colour makes you feel better,' she explains.

Alongside Celia Birtwell, and other leading designers of print in the 1960s such as Bill Gibb and Bernard Nevill, Zandra Rhodes was responsible for the diverse multi-patterned look that defined an era of exuberant self-expression in the 1960s, when design creativity was at a premium. Phillip de Leon points out that 'the explosion of prints in the 1960s was a reflection of the freedom and cultural liberation that the population as a whole was experiencing. Fashion today is obsessed with that decade and the decade that followed. The industry has copied it and romanticized it in every way possible. It was a time of free expression, a celebration of individuality, and though we are just as free now to express and create (if not more so) there was a rebelliousness tied to that era that we are constantly trying to evoke.'

During that era Zandra Rhodes produced many innovative ideas that were to influence a generation of print designers. Her tattoo print transfers and paper dresses were as significant as her early use of the logo as a design motif, and her use of unusual subject matter for print ideas, such as the lipstick print. She produced her first collection of clothes under her own label in 1969, a mixture of historical and tribal influences that typified the developing hippie culture, and that was to prove her signature style.

-Mademoiselles-
Best Friend

The Californian company Alexander Henry Fabrics has an
archive of thousands of designs dating from the 1960s. The
head designers Phillip and Nicole de Leon rework these
vintage designs to produce prints that have a contemporary
edge while retaining their original integrity.

Zandra Rhodes' ability to combine colour, pattern and garment shape into a cohesive and exotic whole is amply seen in this 'Indian Feather Sunspray' dress from 1970.

During the minimalism of the late 1980s and 1990s her fantasy gowns – embellished with beads, sequins and feathers, and with a free-floating silhouette – found less favour with a fashion press preoccupied with the severe structures and precision cutting of Prada and Gucci. However, the contemporary desire for a more joyful relationship with colour and pattern is exactly fulfilled by the Rhodes look.

Jane Shepherdson, brand director of Britain's leading retail empire Topshop, recognized that the time was right for a reappraisal of Rhodes's work in terms of a contemporary audience. She successfully incorporated a range of garments into the stores, as well as sponsoring a retrospective exhibition of the designer's work at the Fashion and Textile Museum in London, titled 'A Lifelong Love Affair with Textiles'. 'We felt that there was a generation that didn't know of Zandra's work, who would love it if it was styled in a way that they could wear with jeans. We were right!'

The designer's inspiration is rooted in the use of autographic sketchbooks (visual equivalent of the autobiography), often compiled on her travels, or by sourcing images from nature. 'I still work from my sketchbooks. That's the only lead into my creativity.' She then transforms the initial drawings into the loose, flowing forms that play with scale and vibrant colour combinations, often including the instantly recognizable 'squiggle'. Rhodes still prefers the established methods of printing: 'I only do screen printing in the traditional manner.'

She is happiest when the trend in fashion coincides with her love of vernacular dress, so that the construction of the garments can reflect the simple shapes that are both functional and use the whole width of the fabric. 'I had come across the actual chronicle of costume, the definitive book by Max Tilke on *Costume Patterns and Designs*. This book was infinitely appealing to me, with its simple and detailed pages showing the cut and form of traditional clothing from around the world. Details of armholes, wrapped trousers, embroidered waistcoats and flat, worked out kaftan and peasant shapes were all explained with the simplicity of a gardening book. It was far more exciting and informative than the edicts of Paris couture.'[viii]

However, as she says now, 'the silhouette has to follow fashion. If ethnic fashion isn't a trend then garments have to be cut closer to the body. The only constant thing in fashion is change, but you have to stay true to yourself even when fashion is against you.' The garment shapes maximize the effect of the print, relying on layers, gathers,

Images from the wall of Zandra Rhodes' studio, based at the Fashion and Textile Museum, a resource and educational centre in London.

smocking, and shirring and often featuring handkerchief points. The clothes are engineered to accommodate the placement of the print rather than cut from continuous repetitive yardage. 'Print influences the shape. You could cut out one of my garments without having a dress pattern because the print indicates where to cut.'

In 2003 Rhodes realized a long-held ambition and opened the Fashion and Textile Museum in Bermondsey on London's South Bank. Designed by Brazilian architect Ricardo Legorreta, its strikingly coloured frontage has become a showcase for contemporary and vintage textile design. In recent years Zandra Rhodes has also become subject to a revival of interest in her work. As the designer explains, 'I have a distinctive style, which can work for me or against me. When it's with you, it's great. My book, *The Art of Zandra Rhodes*, which came out in 1984, is a major influence on other designers, and I looked at all the print around recently and thought, if everyone is knocking me off, I should knock myself off.'

Her personal style reflects the flamboyant quality of her clothes; her hair is pink, and her use of cosmetics distinctive. 'I have a point of view and if I want to change it then I have to do it gradually and still give people what they expect. Certain things are expected of me.'

The cyclical nature of fashion ensures that print designs from previous eras come round not once, but time and again, just as fashion itself reappraises, reinvents and frankly copies garments from the past. Prints are integral to the garment, and the surface pattern will inevitably reflect the period in which it was made. A square-shouldered, tie-fronted 1940s blouse will not be made up of fabric printed with the large-scale modular prints of the 1960s. Print and cut carry the same resonance. Society does not move forward in smooth progression, but accelerates and slows down and even regresses. Even if there is at times a reluctance to engage with the past, there are also times when there is greater reluctance to engage with the future. Designers of print for fashion tap into this need for the reassurance of the familiar, or may simply reappraise and remodel their sources into rampant modernity. There is clearly a difference between 'reworking' an image to give it a contemporary resonance, and celebrating the rarity of a vintage print by wearing it as it is. There used to be a saying that styles skipped a generation, that what was worn by a parent would be neglected by the children but be newly attractive to the grandchildren. Allowing for the speed of changing fashions, ten years is now considered vintage, and fashion and print revivals occur with ever more frequency.

footnotes

CHAPTER 2 AND, NEXT TO NATURE, ART

i   Christopher Breward, *The Culture of Fashion: A New History of Fashionable Dress* (Manchester: Manchester University Press, 1995, p. 126).

ii Elizabeth Wilson, *The Sphinx in the City: Urban Life, the Control of Disorder, and Women* (London: Virago, 1991; Berkeley: University of California Press, 1992, p. 26).

iii Li Edelkoort, *Bloom Book: Horticulture for the 21st century* (Paris: Flammarion, 2001, p. 183).

iv Pastoureau, Michel, *The Devil's Cloth: A History of Stripes and Striped Fabric*, translated by Jody Gladding (New York: Columbia University Press, 2001, p. 24).

v   *Grazia* magazine, 20 June 2005, pp. 22–24.

vi Andrew Bolton, *Wild: Fashion Untamed* (New York: Metropolitan Museum of Art, and New Haven, Connecticut: Yale University Press, 2004, p. 120).

vii Hardy Blechman, *D P M: Disruptive Pattern Material*, vol. 1: *An Encyclopaedia of Camouflage in Nature, Warfare, and Culture* (London: D P M, and Richmond Hill, Ontario: Firefly, 2004, pp. 450–52).

CHAPTER 3 ABSTRACT

i   E H Gombrich, *The Sense of Order: A Study in the Psychology of Decorative Art* (The Wrightsman Lectures), (Oxford: Phaidon, and Ithaca, N Y: Cornell University Press, 1979, p. 65).

ii A H Christie, *Traditional Methods of Pattern Designing: An Introduction to the Study of the Decorate Art* (Oxford: Clarendon Press, 1910, pp. 26–44).

iii Lesley Jackson, *20th-Century Pattern Design: Textile & Wallpaper Pioneers* (London: Mitchell Beazley, and New York: Princeton Architectural Press, 2002, pp. 44–55).

CHAPTER 4 FOLKLORE, FANTASY AND FABLE

i   Christie, op. cit., p. 46.
ii   Eric Hobsbawn, *The Age of Revolution: Europe 1789–1814* (London: Weidenfeld & Nicolson, 1962; New York: Praeger, 1969, p. 266).
iii   Jackson, op. cit., p. 47.
iv   *Sunday Times Style* magazine, 22 August 2004, p. 25.
v   Gombrich, op. cit.
vi   Stuart Robinson, *History of Printed Textiles* (London: Studio Vista, and Cambridge, M A: M I T Press, 1969)
vii   *Vogue*, March 2005, pp. 198
viii   Robinson, op. cit.
ix   *Vogue*, May 2005, p.208

CHAPTER 5 GRAPHICS AND GRAFFITI

i   John Berger, *Ways of Seeing* (London: British Broadcasting Corporation and Penguin Books, 1972; New York: Viking, 1973, p. 129).
ii   Obey Clothing Company, *I-D* magazine.
iii   Pastoureau, op. cit.
iv   Ibid., p 2.
v   Marnie Fogg, *Boutique: A 60s Cultural Phenomenon* (London: Mitchell Beazley, 2003, p. 144).

CHAPTER 6 VINTAGE

i   *W*, August 1996, p.171.
ii   *Times* magazine, 25 June 2005, p. 54.
iii   *Harpers & Queen*, February 2005, pp. 43–46.
iv   Quoted in Shirley Kennedy, *Pucci: A Renaissance in Fashion* (New York: Abbeville, 1991, p. 113).
v   *Elle Decoration* magazine, July 2005, p. 19.
vi   Diane von Furstenberg, *Diane: A Signature Life* (New York: Simon & Schuster, 1998, p. 74).
vii   Diane von Furstenberg, *Diane von Furstenberg's Book of Beauty* (New York: Simon & Schuster, 1976, p. 33).
viii   Zandra Rhodes with Anne Knight, *The Art of Zandra Rhodes* (London: Cape, 1984; Boston: Houghton Mifflin, 1985, p. 37).

bibliography

Baines, Barbara Burman, *Fashion Revivals: From the Elizabethan Age to the Present Day*, Batsford, London 1981.

Bender, Marylin, *The Beautiful People*, Coward McCann, New York 1967

Berger, John, *Ways of Seeing*, British Broadcasting Corporation and Penguin Books, London 1972 and Viking, New York 1973.

Blanchard, Tamsin, *Fashion and Graphics*, Laurence King Publishing, London 2004.

Blechman, Hardy, *DPM Disruptive Pattern Material, An Encyclopaedia of Camouflage in: Nature, Warfare and Culture*, DPM and Richmond Hill, London and Firefly, Ontario 2004.

Bolton, Andrew, *Wild: Fashion Untamed*, Metropolitan Museum of Art and New Haven Connecticut, Yale University Press, New York 2004.

Breward, Christopher, *The Culture of Fashion, A New History of Fashionable Dress* Manchester University Press, Manchester 1995.

Breward, Christopher, *Fashion*, Oxford University Press, Oxford 2003.

Christie, A. H. *Traditional Methods of Pattern Designing: An Introduction to the Study of Decorative Art*, Clarendon Press, Oxford 1910.

Craik, Jennifer, *The Face of Fashion: Cultural Studies in Fashion*, Routledge, London 1993.

Edelkoort, Li, *Bloom Book: Horticulture for the 21st century*, Flammarion, Paris 2001
Fogg, Marnie, *Boutique: A 60s Cultural Phenomenon*, Mitchell Beazley, London 2003

Gombrich, E.H. *The Sense of Order, A Study in the Psychology of Decorative Art*, (The Wrightsman Lectures) Phaidon, 1979

Hobsbawm, E, *The Age of Revolution Europe 1789-1814*, London Weidenfeld & Nicolson, London 1995

Jackson, Leslie, *20th-Century Pattern Design, Textile and Wallpaper Pioneers*, Mitchell Beazley, London 2002

Kennedy, Shirley, *Pucci: A Renaissance in Fashion*, Abbeville, New York 1991

Pastoureau, Michel, *The Devil's Cloth. A History of Stripes and Striped Fabric*, (translated by Jody Gladding), New York Columbia University Press, 2001.

Rhodes, Zandra with Knight, Anne, *The Art of Zandra Rhodes*, Cape, London 1984 and Houghton Mifflin, Boston 1985.

Rhodes, Zandra, *A Lifelong Love affair with Textiles*, Antique Collectors' Club Ltd and Zandra Rhodes Publications Ltd, 2005

Robinson, Stuart, *A History of Printed Textiles*, London Studio Vista and Cambridge M A: M I T Press, 1969.

Smith, Paul, *You Can Find Inspiration in Anything(and if you can't, look again!)*, Violette Editions, London 2001.

Spurling, Hilary, *Matisse the Master*, Hamish Hamilton, London 2005

Tucker, Andrew, *Dries van Noten: Shape, Print and Fabric*, Thames & Hudson, London 1999.

Von Furstenberg, Diane, *Diane: A Signature Life*, Simon & Schuster, New York 1998.

Von Fusrtenberg, Diane, *Book of Beauty* Simon & Schuster, New York 1976.

Wilson, Elizabeth, *The Sphinx in the City: Urban Life, the Control of Disorder, and Women*, Virago London 1991 and University of California Press, Berkley 1992

index

Page references in *italics*
refer to illustrations

A

Abstract Expressionism 65
Accornero, Vittoria 27
Adeyemi, Wale 137
Aesthetic Movement 50
Adidas 137
age of gold 159
Aldrich, Larry 65
Alexander Henry Fabrics 7,
    11, 12, 101, 102, 106, 107,
    131, 144, 145, 157, 172,
    173
Antwerp Fashion Academy
    119
'Antwerp Six' 119
Anuszkiewicz, Richard 65
Appleyard, Brigitte 10, *17*
Aquascutum 11
Art Deco 9, 65, 163
Art Nouveau 9, 28, 50, 124,
    163
Arts and Crafts Movement
    28, 41, 159
Asprey 22
Atelier Martine 103

B

Bailey, Christopher 8, *158,*
    158, 168
Bakst, Leon 168
Ballet Russes 168
Barber, Noel 164
Bartley Luella *65, 66, 67,*
    75, 129, 137
Basquiat Jean-Michel 137
Basso & Brooke 17, *18,* 19,
    120, *121, 122, 123,* 124,
    126, 127

Basso, Bruno 17, 120
batik 108
Bauhaus 77, 104
Beardsley, Aubrey 127
The Beatles 147
Beckham, David 137
Belford, Patricia 19, 20, 60,
    86
Belford Prints Ltd 19
Bellucci, Monica 54
Berger, John 130
Bigwood, Fleet 10, 11, 13,
    16, *16, 17,* 85
Birtwell, Celia 10, 13, 28,
    93, 124, 168, 169, *169,*
    170, 171
Blake, Peter 147
Blechman, Hardy 54
block printing 9, 27,
    108,110, 112
Bodymap 10
Bottega Veneta 127
Brando, Marlon 135
Brody, Neville 10
Brooke, Christopher 120
Brown, Barbara 68
Burberry 8, 135, 158
Burberry Prorsum 8, 159
Brunschweiler factory 108

C

Cacharel 11, 120, 150, 168
calico 27
Calicut 27
Camberwell College of Art,
    London 86, 155
camouflage 52, 54, *55, 56,*
    57, 58, 59
Carhartt 137
Castiglioni, Consuelo 8, 13,
    118

Cavalli, Eva 53
Cavalli, Roberto 53
cave paintings 46, 52
Centre for Advanced
    Textiles, Glasgow School of
    Art 77
Central St Martins School
    of Art 16, 77, 81, 92, 96,
    120, 135, 148, 150
Ceprynski, Ann 50, 52
Chalayan, Hussein *32,* 33,
    93
Chanel 132, 162
Cheap Date 161
Chloe
Christensen, Helena 50
Christie, A.H. 103
Clark, Ossie 10, 93, 124,
    168
Clements Ribiero 119, 120
Clements, Suzanne 119,
    168
Commes des Garcons 10
Conran, Jasper 11, 20,
Convention on
    International trade in
    Endangered Species 53
'conversational prints' 81
Cosmopolitan 164
Crichton, Rory 2, *34, 35,*
    48, *60, 65, 66, 67,* 74, *75,*
    77, *126, 127,* 127, *129,*
Crosland, Neisha 21, *63, 84,*
    85, 85, 86, 89, *89,* 90, 92
Cubism 65

D

Dazed & Confused 150
Deacon, Giles 74, 124
Dean, James 135
Decades 156

Defoe, Daniel 27
Delaunay, Sonia 65
De Leon, Marc 11
De Leon, Nicole 11, 12, 14
De Leon, Phillip 11, 12, 14, 169
Demeulemeester, Ann 119
devoré printing 20
Dietrich, Marlene 163
digital printing 14, 17, 19, 19, 21, 22, 39, 50, 89, 92, 124, 142, 147
Dior, Christian 132, 135
discharge printing 13, 22, 143
Dolce & Gabbana 24, 53
D:P:M: Disruptive Pattern Material 54

E
e-bay 159
E-commerce 130
Edelkoort, Li 31
Edinburgh Weavers 68
Eley Kishimoto 13, 16, 55, 64, 92, 92, 93, 93, 94, 95, 96, 97, 98, 99, 110, 111, 111
Eley, Mark 13, 92, 93, 96
Emilioform 164
Emin, Tracy 132
English East India Company 27
Escher, M.C 81
Etro 13, 107

F
The Face 150
Fake London 57
Fashion & Textile Museum, Bermondsey, London

174, 176
Fellini, Frederico 53
First State Textile Factory, Moscow 65
'flower power' 28
Ford, Tom 10
Forrer, Robert 108
Frostfrench 154, 155
Furphy-Simpson Studio 13, 14, 105, 181
Furphy, Val 13
Future Laboratory 8
Futurism 65

G
Galliano, John 57, 103, 104, 134, 150, 158
Gardner, Ava 53
Garnett, Bay 160, 161
Gaultier, John-Paul 103
Giannini, Frida 27
Gibb, Bill 10, 169
Gibo 23, 150, 155
Gibson, Natalie 96
Gieves & Hawkes 60
Giles 2, 34, 35, 60
Ginka 85, 86, 86, 87, 88, 89, 90
Givenchy 117
Glasgow School of Art 77, 127
Ghost 150
Gombrich, E.H. 64, 107
Griffiths, Amanda 27
Graffiti 136, 138
Grand, Katie 135
Gropius, Walter 77
Gucci 10, 27, 48, 74, 77, 127, 174
Gucci, Rodolpho 27

H
Haeckel, Ernst 92
Hamilton, Richard 81
Hamnett, Katherine 10
Haring Keith 137
Hartley, Nick 39
Hayworth, Rita 53
Heals 68
Hepburn, Audrey 163, 164
Hesiod 159
Hicks, Allegra 46, 46, 47, 48, 48, 49, 158
Hill, Sandra 140
Hillson, Bobby 148
Hindmarch, Anya 132, 133
Hobsbawm, E. 103
Hodgson, Sarah 146, 147, 148, 149
Hoon, Jenny 110

I
Indigo 40
Industrial Revolution 28

J
Jackson, Betty 19
Jacobs, Marc 27, 93, 137, 156, 158
Jagger, Jade 50
Joliffe, Kira 161
Jung, Carl 120

K
kaftan 46
Kahlo, Frida 103
Kaikai Kiki Corporatoion 132
Kakanias, Konstantin 13
Karan, Donna 10, 16, 19, 20
Kashmir 107

Kawakubo, Rei 10
Kelly, Grace 27, 163
Kennedy, Jackie 163, 164
Kenzo 117

Kiely, Orla 68, *69, 70, 71, 72, 73*
Kishimoto, Wakako 13, 16, 92, 93
Klein Calvin 10, 19
Kozhikode 27
Krenek, Carl 65

L
Lacroix, Christian 13, 165
La Dolce Vita 54
Landor, W.S. 27
Lang, Helmut 147
Law, Natasha *38,* 41, 148, *154,* 155
Legorreta, Ricardo 176
Liberty 10, 28
Liberty, Arthur Lasenby 28
London College of Fashion 150
London Fashion Week 39, 124
Lou Lou and Law 41
Luella *see* Bartley, Luella
L.V.M.H. (Louis Vuitton-Moet Hennessey) 164

M
McCartney, Stella 108
McQueen, Alexander 81, 93
Maharishi 54
Mali 108
Margiela, Martin 10, 119
Marimekko 28
Marni 8, 12, 13, *118,* 118,

161
Matisse 46, 168, 169
Medway College (the Kent Institute) 150
Michael, Anthony 135
Mighall, Magnus 17
Missoni 142, 143, 146
Missoni, Angela 147
Missoni, Rosita 143
Missoni, Tai 143
Miu Miu 68, *68*
Modernism 163
Mondrian, Piet 64
Monroe, Marilyn 164
Morris, William 28, 86
Moss, Kate 50, 161
Mucha, Alphonse 124
Murakami, Takashi 132

N
Nash, Stephanie 135
Nevill Bernard 9, 169
Newsweek 167
New York School of Visual Arts 137
New York Textile Museum 12
Nihon–ga 132
Noki 136

O
Op Art 9, 65, 147
Osborne & Little 8 9
Ottoman Empire 89

P
paisley 10, 104, *105,* 107
Pantone Colour System 118
Park, Megan 14, *15,* 112, *113, 114, 115, 116, 117,* 117, 118

peacock feather 10, 50, 52, 104
Philip, Stephen 156, 162, 163
Picasso 86
pigment dyeing 20
Pisanello 60
Poiret, Paul 9, 103
Pollock, Jackson 81
Pop art 9, 67, 147, 163
Posen, Zac 111
Prada 119, 147, 174
Prada, Miuccia 68, 108
Premier Vision 13, 40
Proust 46
Psychedelia 9, 28, 50, 135, 150
Pucci 9, 13, 81, 74, 81, 147, *163,* 163, 164, *165,* 167, 168
Pucci, Laudomia 165
Pucci, Marquis Emilio
Pucci di Barsento 164
Puma 137
Punk 163

R
Radiolaria 92
R.A.Smart 17
Raymond, Martin 8, 9, 112
reactive acid dyes 20, 142
Reflective Technology Industries 130
Reid, Jamie 135
Rellik 156, *162,* 162, *163*
resist dyeing 108
Rhodes, Zandra 10, 13, 169, 174, *175, 177*

Ribiero, Inacio 19, 168
Riley, Bridget 65
Roberts, Tommy 135
Rodriguez, Narciso 11
roller printing 9
Romantic period 159
Rossellini, Isabella 54
Roswald, Ann-Louise 24,
    25, 36, 37, 38, 39, *39*, 40,
    40, 41, 41, *42, 43, 44, 45*,
    161
rotary printing 143
Rotten, Johnny 135
Royal College of Art 9, 147
The Rug Company 140
Russian Expressionism 86

S
Sage, Russell 135
Saint Laurent, Yves 13, 64,
    93
Sander, Jill 11, 93
Saunders, Jonathan *4*, 22,
    65, *76, 77*, 77, *78, 79, 80*,
    81, *82, 83*, 92
Savile Row 60
Schlemmer, Oscar 77
screen printing 9, 16, *16, 17*,
    19, *20, 21, 22*, 22, 39, *39*,
    41, 48, 50, 93, 130, 136,
    142
Sex pistols 135
*Sgt Pepper's Lonely Hearts
Club Band* 147
Shakespeare, William 27,
    60
Shepherdson, Jane 12, 13,
    174
shibori-an 108
Silver, Cameron 156
Simon, Samuel 9

Simpson, Ian 13
'smart' dyes 22
Smith, Hilde 10
Smith, Paul *26, 28, 29, 30,
    31*, 138, *141*
Spenser, Edmund 27
Sprouse, Stephen, 54, 137,
    165
St Francis 60
Stepanova, Varvara 65
stripes 52, *138*, 138, 143,
    146
Stussy 137
The Sunday Times 150
Surrealism 124
Swarovski 124

T
Tangye, Howard 150
Tattoos 106
Teller, Juergen 160
Thatcher, Margaret 135,
    138
thermocratic inks 22
thrifting 161
tie-dyeing 108, 135
Tilke, Max 174
tjanting tool 108
Tomchin, Julian 65
Tootal Batik 108
Topshop 12, 174
Treacy, Philip 150
Triadic Ballet 77
Tyler, Richard 150

U
University of Ulster 19

V
Van Noten, Dries 12, 13,
    117, 119, *119*

Vasarely, Victor 81
Verhoeven, Julie 23, 132,
    148, 150, *151, 152, 153*
Versace, Gianni 10, 165
Victoria & Albert Museum
    86, 150
Viewpoint 8
Vision of St Eustace 60
Vogue 161
Von Furstenberg, Diane
    166, 167, 168
Vorticism 65
Vuitton, Georges 132
Vuitton, Louis 93, 132, 135,
    137

W
Walters & Sons, Stephen
    127
Warhol, Andy 54, 132
Weekly Review 27
Westwood, Vivienne 10, 19
Whitehead, David 68
Wiener Werkstatte 65, 103
Williamson, Matthew 19,
    21, 24, *50*, 50,
    52, 161
Wimmer-Wisgrill, Eduard
    Josef 65

Y
Yamamoto, Yohji 10

Z
Zara 12

acknowledgements

To John, and in memory of my mother, Trudy Fogg.

Thanks to Helen Evans and Tina Persaud at B T Batsford; Emily Angus, Allan Hutchings, Allegra Hicks, Ann Ceprynski, Ann-Louise Roswald, Anya Hindmarch, Bay Garnett, Bernard Nevill, Brigitte Appleyard, Bruno Basso and Christopher Brooke of Basso & Brooke, Burberry, Caroline Cox, Celia Birtwell, Christopher Bailey, Christopher Laszlo, Consuelo Castiglioni of Marni, Diane Von Furstenberg, Fleet Bigwood, Frank McEwan, Gavin Joule at Ann-Louise Roswald, Giles Deacon, Hussein Chalayan, Jane Shepherdson, Jenelle Hamilton and Tracy Le Marquand at Karla Otto, Jenny Hoon, Jonathan Saunders, Joyce Vigar, Julie Verhoeven, Kate Southworth at Anya Hindmarch, Liza Wood and Emma Lucas at Camera Press, Luella, Magnus Mighall at R.A. Smart, Mark Eley and Wakako Kishimoto of Eley Kishimoto, Marsha Ilsley at Burberry, Martin Raymond of Future Laboratory, Matthew Williamson, Megan Park, Natalie Abram at Orla Kiely, Natasha Law, Neisha Crosland, Nicole de Leon of Alexander Henry Fabrics, Niki Diamond, Noki, Orla Kiely, Pam Hemmings, Patricia Belford, Sir Paul Smith, Phillip de Leon of Alexander Henry Fabrics, Rekha Sidhu at LUCHFORD APM, Richard Clarke and colleagues at the University of Derby Learning Centre, Rory Crichton, Rowena Hamilton, Russell Sage, Sandra Hill and Davina Waide at Paul Smith, Sarah Hodgson, Tom Trinkle at Maharishi, Steven Phillip of Rellik, Val Furphy & Ian Simpson of Furphy-Simpson Studio, Zandra Rhodes.

picture credits

Pages: 2 Rory Crichton; 5 Chris Moore; 7 Alexander Henry Fabrics; 8 Marni; 11 Burberry Prorsum; 12 Alexander Henry Fabrics; 14 Furphy-Simpson Studio; 15 Megan Park; 16–17 Allan Hutchings; 18 Basso & Brooke; 19–23 Allan Hutchings; 24 Gavin Joule for Ann-Louise Roswald; 26–31 Paul Smith. 32 Hussein Chalayan; 34–35 Rory Crichton; 36–39 Gavin Joule for Ann-Louise Roswald; 40–41 Ann-Louise Roswald; 42–45 Gavin Joule for Ann-Louise Roswald; 46–49 Allegra Hicks; 50–51 Matthew Williamson; 52 Burberry Prorsum; 53 Chris Moore; 55 Eley Kishimoto; 56 Neil Davenport for Maharishi; 58–59 Maharishi; 60–61 Rory Crichton; 62–63 Neisha Crosland; 64 Eley Kishimoto; 65–67 Rory Crichton; 68 Chris Moore; 69–73 Orla Kiely; 75 Rory Crichton; 76–83 Jonathan Saunders; 84 Neisha Crosland; 85–86 Allan Hutchings; 88 Neisha Crosland; 89 Allan Hutchings; 90–91 Neisha Crosland; 92–99 Eley Kishimoto; 100–102 Alexander Henry Fabrics; 105 Furphy-Simpson Studio; 106–107 Alexander Henry Fabrics; 108–109 John Angus; 110-111 Eley Kishimoto; 113–117 Jane McLeish-Kelsey (Megan Park design); 118 Marni; 119 Dries Van Noten; 121–125 Basso & Brooke; 126–9 Rory Crichton; 130 Alexander Henry Fabrics; 133 Anya Hindmarch; 134 Kate Barry; 136 Noki; 138–141 Paul Smith; 142 Alessandro Zeno/Scope; 144–145 Alexander Henry Fabrics;146–149 Sarah Hodgson, 151–153 Julie Verhoeven; 154 Natasha Law; Natasha Law, courtesy of Space; 156–157 Alexander Henry Fabrics; 158–159 Burberry Prorsum; 160 courtesy of Bay Garnett; 162–165 Allan Hutchings; 166 Roger Prigent courtesy of Diane von Furstenberg Studio; 169 Celia Birtwell/*Another Magazine*; 170–171 Celia Birtwell; 172–173 Alexander Henry Fabrics; 175–177 Zandra Rhodes; 190-191 Furphy-Simpson Studio.

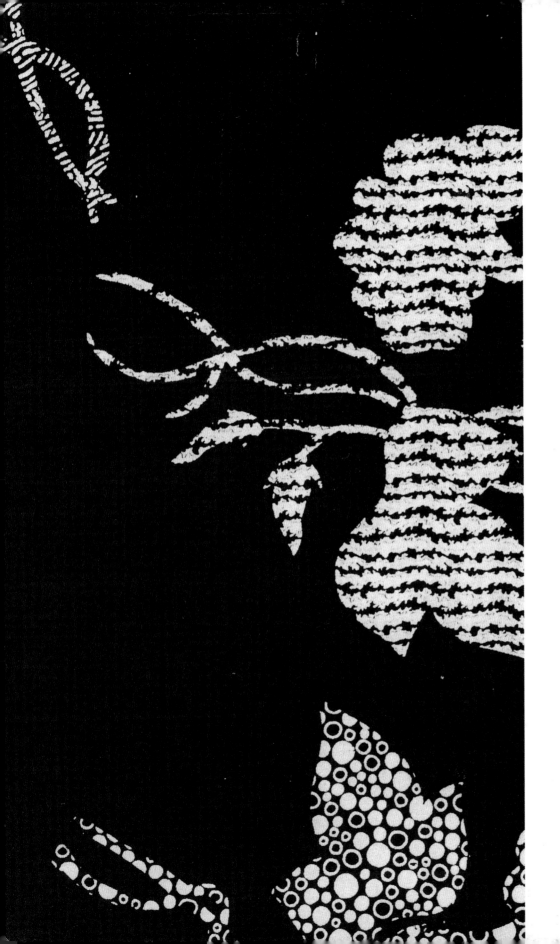